KU-285-285

IN SEARCH OF INDIA AND HER NEIGHBOURS

IN SEARCH

OF

INDIA AND HER NEIGHBOURS

PUBLISHED BY THE READER'S DIGEST ASSOCIATION LIMITED

LONDON   NEW YORK   MONTREAL   SYDNEY   CAPE TOWN

Originally published in partwork form,
Des Pays et des Hommes,
by Librairie Larousse, Paris

A Reader's Digest selection

IN SEARCH OF INDIA AND HER NEIGHBOURS

First English Edition Copyright © 1993
The Reader's Digest Association Limited, Berkeley Square House,
Berkeley Square, London W1X 6AB

Copyright © 1993
Reader's Digest Association Far East Limited
Philippines Copyright 1993
Reader's Digest Association Far East Limited

All rights reserved

Originally published in French as a partwork,
Des Pays et des Hommes
Copyright © 1991
Librairie Larousse
All rights reserved

Translated and edited by Toucan Books Limited, London
Translated and adapted by Andrew Kerr-Jarrett and Alex Martin

No part of this book may be reproduced, stored in a retrieval system
or transmitted in any form or by any means, electronic, electrostatic,
magnetic tape, mechanical, photocopying, recording or otherwise,
without permission in writing from the publishers

® Reader's Digest, The Digest and the Pegasus logo
are registered trademarks of
The Reader's Digest Association Inc. of Pleasantville, New York, USA

ISBN 0 276 42054 3

Printed by Printer Industria Gráfica S.A., Barcelona

Contents

COVER PICTURES

Top: *The towering peaks of the Himalayas form the northern border of Nepal;
the area is known as 'the Roof of the World' and includes
the world's highest mountain, Everest.*

Bottom: *Brass and earthenware pots containing water are balanced on the
heads of women in Ranakpur, Rajasthan, India.*

New Nations in Ancient Lands

'You may take it for a fact,' wrote Marco Polo in his *Travels*, 'that India is the richest and most splendid province in the world. . . . Everything there is different from what it is with us and excels both in size and beauty.' He goes on to catalogue the country's natural and mineral wealth: pepper, ginger, cinnamon, indigo, brazilwood, pearls, rubies, coconuts, cotton, as well as black lions, parrots of many kinds and 'peacocks much bigger and handsomer than ours'. He admires the leatherwork of Gujarat, 'embossed with birds and beasts and stitched with gold and silver of very fine workmanship, so exquisite that they are a marvel to behold'. Trade thrives, with exports of spices and manufactures to Arabia and imports of brass and horses, cloth of gold and silk, silver, cloves and spikenard. 'You must know that ships come here from very many parts, notably from the great province of Manzi (S. China), and goods are exported to many parts. Those that go to Aden are carried from there to Alexandria.' Polo also found much to commend in the government and religion of the people, as well as in their diet and general health.

His account, written in 1298, may come as a surprise to a 20th-century reader. We have become accustomed to thinking of India as a poor country, a straggler in the world economic race, hampered by primitive agriculture and inefficient industry, struggling against over-population, illiteracy, malnutrition and disease. Yet, as the following pages show, the splendours of India are not all in the past. Its wealth – measured not in bare economic terms but in its wildlife and natural beauty, its crafts, its trades, its religious and cultural traditions – remains vast.

The origins of Indian culture go back to the Indus or Harappan civilisation that flourished between 2300 and 1750 BC in the north-west of the country. The remains of the Harappan culture are found over a huge area – almost 500,000 square miles – covering all of modern Pakistan and Punjab. There are over 70 archaeological sites, including the cities of Harappa, Mohenjo-daro and Kali-Banga whose populations are estimated to have been 30-40,000 each. They reveal a written language (still undeciphered), urban sanitation, standardised weights and measures, trade with Mesopotamia, Iran and the Persian Gulf, a transport system that used land, river and sea, high-quality buildings in brick, workshops of metal workers, potters and dyers, grain-stores, houses with bathrooms, the cultivation of cotton, wheat, rice, barley, melons, peas and dates, and the domestication of a wide range of animals.

Around 1700 BC this civilisation declined, perhaps because of geological or environmental changes (the advance of the deserts, the shifting courses of rivers), and a new civilisation appeared further east along the Ganges river, coinciding with the incursions from Central Asia of an Indo-European race speaking a language that was the source not only of Sanskrit but also of Latin and Greek. Out of this Ganges civilisation came the earliest Indian sacred texts, the *Vedas,* and from them the Hindu religion. The 6th century BC saw the birth of two more Indian religions, Buddhism and Jainism. The first Indian empire, ruling almost the whole subcontinent, evolved under the Maurya dynasty (4th to 2nd century BC). The Maurya kings were in diplomatic contact with the successors of Alexander the Great, whose armies had reached the Punjab in 327 BC. Mauryan society was divided into castes and organised with great financial and administrative efficiency. The most notable king was Asoka (273-232 BC) a convert to Buddhism. His edicts, carved on stone columns found the length and breadth of India, preach a remarkable philosophy of non-violence, mercy to animals, and tolerance, generosity and mutual respect among all the ranks and individuals of society. Cynical historians trace the decline of the Mauryan power to this 'gentle' philosophy, but for whatever cause the empire soon broke up into a series of smaller kingdoms. Many of these continued to trade extensively overseas, with regular contacts spread as far as China and Rome. Christianity is said to have reached India with the arrival of St Thomas in the middle of the 1st century AD.

Other empires have come and gone: the Guptas (AD 320-540), whose rule is called India's 'Classical Age', the Delhi sultanate, founded by Muslim conquerors in the late 12th century: the Vijayanagar Empire in the South (1336-1646); the Mogul Empire (1526-1761), the Marathas (1627-1817), and of course the Portuguese and the British.

The arrival of Vasco da Gama at Calicut in 1498 renewed India's lapsed contacts with Europe. It opened up irresistible commercial prospects for the well-armed western traders: first the Portuguese, then the Dutch, the French and the British. Military and colonial power was installed afterwards, as a protection for commercial interests.

The British presence in India, which lasted from 1600 to 1947, was inspired by motives that grew in complexity as time went on. The simple desire for profit grew into a need for self-protection and the elimination of rivals, then a quest for administrative efficiency and improved communications, until the British found themselves – after the Indian Mutiny of 1857 – taking over the running of practically the entire country. The missionary zeal that accompanied this growing entanglement included not only Christian evangelism but also the gospel of technology, progress, education. We can see now why that process was bound to lead to independence – which was finally achieved in 1947 after a struggle lasting over 50 years.

The histories of most of the neighbouring states – Pakistan, Nepal, Bangladesh, Burma (now officially called Myanmar), Sri Lanka and the Maldives – also feature periods of British domination. Pakistan and Bangladesh formed parts of the various Indian empires, including the British, until 1947. They were then separated from India and existed as West and East Pakistan until 1971, when war broke out between them. In 1972 they became Pakistan and Bangladesh. Nepal under the Shah dynasty (1769-1951) reached an arrangement with the British guaranteeing Nepalese independence and security in exchange for the right to recruit Gurkha soldiers for the Indian Army and to influence foreign policy. This was just one of many successful balancing acts achieved by the kings of Nepal between their own interests and those of their powerful neighbours to the north and south. Burma was conquered by the British in three separate wars over the period 1824-1885, aimed at securing trade to China through the back door. The Burmese – a separate people in every way from the Indians, with their own civilisations going back to the 4th century BC – were humiliated by the annexation of their country to India and never fully accepted British rule. The British left Burma in 1948; since then the country has struggled under military dictatorship and mismanagement of the economy, yet its people have lost none of that gentleness, optimism and charm which as one historian put it, 'makes one proud of the human race'.

Sri Lanka (Ceylon until 1972) became a British colony in 1802, taking over from the Dutch East India Company. The Dutch had been invited in to oust the Portuguese, who had first landed in Ceylon in 1505 and gradually taken over control of the island. After independence in 1947, the ancient rivalry of Tamils, based in the north, and Sinhalese, based in the south, was more or less contained until 1981 when Tamil separatists began a guerrilla war which has now continued for more than 10 years. The Maldives, which for centuries fell under the same colonial influences as Ceylon, achieved full independence from Britain in 1965, but have been free of the ethnic conflicts that often boil up so fiercely, worldwide, in the aftermath of Empire.

India

From the snow-clad Himalayas in the north to the lush tropical rain
forests in the south, India's range of landscapes is matched by its
variety of flora and fauna and the diversity of its cultural heritage.
The country with the second largest population in the world is a
complex mix of ancient religions and customs, art and architecture.
It is these that have given India its unique character and have caused
many of its contradictions. Today, perhaps the most striking of these is
the way in which India is fighting a constant battle with poverty in
many areas, but remains a thriving industrial nation.

A man takes his cow to sell at the great livestock fair at Pushkar. This fair is one of the biggest in the whole of India and regularly features 100,000 camels, not to mention cows, buffaloes, goats and sheep.

Previous page:
Rajasthani women decorate their hands and sometimes their feet with henna. The designs, which the women create for each other, are supposed to bring good luck. The motifs start with a simple geometrical figure such as a circle or a triangle; flowers and leaves are then added to create an intricate, lively design.

India lives by the rhythm of the monsoons, the source of both life and death. The rain comes every year, but it is capricious and unreliable. Sometimes it comes late, sometimes early, and sometimes too plentifully. Nevertheless, the Indians adapt to it very well. Here, in the streets of Benares, life carries on despite the flooding, and the cycle-rickshaws continue to ply their trade.

The Plains of India

The northern plain is the granary of the subcontinent. Its fertile soil has attracted settlers since the earliest times. Today something like three-quarters of the population live there, many of whom scratch a harsh existence from tiny plots of land. The plain is vast, stifling in summer and overpopulated. Yet it does not form a single homogeneous unit; it is best seen as two separate areas or bands running west to east.

The first of these, to the north, is the Indo-Gangetic Plain, its northern edge lying along the Himalayan foothills; in its vast sweep, it includes the basins of the three principal rivers of India, the Indus, the Ganges and the Brahmaputra. It stretches from the Khyber Pass on the Afghan–Pakistan border to the farthest reaches of the Brahmaputra at the frontier with Burma in the east.

The plain begins almost as an extension of the main alleys of the grand bazaar in Peshawar. From there it sweeps on round the great Moghul towers of Lahore, then on to the Punjab (the name means 'land of five rivers'), the historic capitals of Delhi and Agra, and the sacred cities of Mathura, Allahabad, and Benares, finally reaching the state of Bihar, West Bengal, Bangladesh and Assam.

Fed by the glaciers of the Himalayas and swollen by the monsoon rains, the Indus, the Ganges and the Brahmaputra irrigate the land. The upper reaches of the Indus twist through a landscape of granite and schist before heading south across the desert plains of Pakistan. The Ganges and the Brahmaputra flow into the plain from west and east respectively, and form a common delta in the endless maze of waterways that cover much of Bengal.

Seen from the air, the central part of the Indo-Gangetic Plain seems one huge tract of farmland, more than 1000 miles wide – a patchwork of green and brown fields, rice paddies and thickets, studded here and there with close-packed village rooftops. Seen from a car, it looks totally different. The villages are no longer occasional ochre spots like dry patches in a lawn, but swarming centres of humanity where buildings are crammed together to occupy the smallest possible space. Every bit of available land is used for cultivation. Bordering the fields are thickets of banyan, mango and pipal trees: a distant memory of the dense forests filled with tigers and deer that covered the region before the arrival of man.

The southern band of the North Indian Plain begins in the west with two deserts, the Kutch and the Thar. These are only deserts in comparison with the overpopulated areas around Agra, Benares and Lucknow. To the Indians of these crowded regions any land that is underpopulated is a desert.

The Pakistani sections of the Thar (the Thal and the Cholistan) are cotton-growing areas watered by the Indus, while the Kutch consists largely of marshlands populated by nomads and birds. The Indian part of the Thar resembles the African Sahel, its villages built around wells and surrounded by fields. Yet the desert enthusiast would not be disappointed. In the Thar they will find camels – often put to work drawing water from the deep wells – and even a few photogenic sand dunes.

The Kutch is in Gujarat, India's westernmost state. The Thar, to the north, occupies around half of Rajasthan – literally 'Land of Kings' – which was named for its great royal cities of Jaisalmer, Bikaner and Jodhpur. Gujarat and Rajasthan are as fertile as the rest of the Indo-Gangetic plain excluding the Punjab, and the majority of the population is rural, as in the country as a whole. The landscape is generally flat and monotonous, changing with the seasons from luxuriant green to desiccated yellow. This monotony is broken by the Aravalli Hills, which rear from the surrounding flatness and run for some 350 miles north-eastwards through Rajasthan, from Udaipur almost as far as Delhi. Though bare in the north, their mineral-rich slopes are forested in the south with a variety of trees including the

Jaisalmer, a metropolis in the desert, is an architectural masterpiece. Note the carefully worked balconies of yellow sandstone, the overhangs and the boxed enclosures which allow the women to look out on the street without being seen. The street sweeper belongs to a caste of Untouchables, the bhangis.

'flames of the forest', so-called because of their incandescent orange winter blossoms. The Aravalli Hills are also the homeland of the warlike Grassias, who successfully resisted conquest by both the Maharajahs and the British.

Both Gujarat and Rajasthan are rich in animal life – partridges, woodcock, cranes, herons, cormorants, rabbits, gazelles, wild boar and many others. The Rajputs, an ancient warrior tribe, were once keen hunters of boar and enjoyed its meat. (Its domestic cousin, a cross between a boar and a pig, is considered unfit for eating except by the Untouchables.) Farther east lies the hilly landscape populated by the Bhils, an agricultural people of tall, tattooed men in white robes, whose women traditionally wear quantities of heavy silver jewellery. Some of the 2.5 million Bhils who form part of India's tribal population live in Rajasthan; the rest in Madhya Pradesh.

Madhya Pradesh is the biggest of the Indian states, roughly three times the size of England. Forty per cent of it is covered in forests – including the Mahadeo Hills, where Kipling's *The Jungle Book* is set. The state is largely undeveloped, with agricultural areas that are only now beginning to expand, little industry, and mineral wealth that is scarcely exploited. The large towns – Bhopal, Ujjain, Mandu and Gwalior – offer a host of artistic treasures, and the 22 temples of Khajuraho boast some of the greatest sculpture in the subcontinent.

A journey south-west from Madhya Pradesh brings the traveller to the port of Bombay. This great metropolis, with its hinterland state of Maharashtra, occupies a strategic and central position – as significant to the subcontinent as the granaries of the north or the peninsular triangle of the south. Bombay is India's financial capital and its leading industrial city, its biggest west-coast port and the economic heart of a huge area stretching from Gujarat in the north to Karnataka in the south.

Marathi, the language of Maharashtra, is closely related to Hindi, which is spoken by around 30 per cent of the Indian population and is the main language in the states of Rajasthan, Uttar Pradesh, Madhya Pradesh, Haryana, Himachal Pradesh and Bihar. Hindi and Marathi are also related to the other major languages of the north such as Punjabi, Sindhi, Gujarati, Urdu and

Two women chat on the doorstep of a house in Nawalgarh in the Shekhawati region of Rajasthan. The town is immediately recognisable by the frescoes which decorate the houses, built in the 18th and 19th centuries by rich merchants who later moved to Bombay or Calcutta.

Bengali. Thus, while Bombay looks both north and south in terms of geography and trade, it remains firmly northern in its language and culture.

Mud huts and sunken palaces

Most of the dwellings in the Indo-Gangetic plain are built of sun-dried bricks. This makes them fragile and a regular prey to the monsoons, although their simple design and the plentiful supply of building material allows them to be repaired or rebuilt easily. Their inhabitants are the rural poor: share-croppers, smallholders or agricultural labourers. Only the mid- to large-scale landowners live in houses constructed from building materials that are common in the West.

Khajuraho, in northern Madhya Pradesh, is an example of a rich village. The houses consist of rooms arranged round a courtyard. They are built of brick, with tile or slate roofs as opposed to the thatch found in poorer dwellings.

Houses in the villages around Bikaner in the Thar desert in Rajasthan might almost be from another continent. They are built of dried mud over a framework of branches, and are small and round with conical roofs, the only exceptions being the large farmhouses, which are built on a rectangular plan – although still in the same materials.

Farther south, towards Jaisalmer, stone is abundant. The local speciality is a handsome yellow sandstone which is skilfully cut to build charming little houses whose walls are painted with geometric designs. Travellers who expect to find only dried mud houses in India are surprised when they come across the wealth of stone in such places as Sam, Ujjlan and Khuri. Loharki,

midway between the two main cities of the Thar, is a curious mixture of the two traditions, with buildings in both sandstone and mud.

One of the finest architectural jewels of the whole of India is the city of Jaisalmer. Sheltering behind huge ramparts are the splendid villas (*havelis*) built by

Jaipur, the capital of Rajasthan, is known as 'the pink town'. This large city, built by the Maharajah Jai Singh at the beginning of the 18th century, is not actually built of pink stone, but is regularly repainted. A few flowers drawn in whitewash brighten the façade, and the blind arches suggest a strong Islamic influence.

merchants who grew rich on the caravan trade between India and Afghanistan. Some of these villas are enormous, with as many as five floors, and façades so richly and intricately carved that they seem like carpets lavishly embroidered in stone.

Throughout Rajasthan, from the Thar desert to the borders of Madhya Pradesh, the village chiefs or *jagirdars* (so called because they were granted fiefs or *jagirs* by the maharajahs) live on huge farms surrounded by high walls – even in the poorest areas. In the rich areas these farms are little short of castles.

One of the most remarkable of these is at Dundlod, between Delhi and Jaipur, and is now a hotel. The first impression is of a medieval fortress, with high ramparts defending a courtyard where villagers of the *jagirdar* would once seek protection in times of danger. Once inside the buildings, you seem to leap forward several centuries into a world of heavily upholstered Victorian luxury, complete with sofas and armchairs, carpets,

The furniture in this Gujarati house is extremely sparse. The simple bed is made of four legs and a wooden frame with strips of cloth or cords stretched over it. There is no mattress because the bed serves as a bench during the day; during the night it will be covered with quilts. The hanging bench seen here is rare in houses, but is often seen in frescoes and paintings.

In Northern India you see barbers and tailors everywhere. This barber from the village of Nathdwara in the south of Rajasthan is wearing the costume of the great plain of Northern India: dhoti, kurta *and a cap.*

moulded plasterwork, mirrors and wall hangings. The contrast with the crude bare earthworks outside is extraordinary.

The area around Dundlod, centred on the town of Shekhavati, is filled with such architectural curiosities. During the 18th century local merchants amassed large fortunes from the caravan trade, especially in wheat and opium, which was produced here and exported to China.

They spent their wealth on luxurious houses, built on a more or less standard plan around two courtyards. The outer courtyard, which had a street entrance, was used for receiving visitors. Shade was provided by canopies held up on sculpted columns. The inner courtyard was strictly private, reserved for the women of the household and close family members. The same double-courtyard plan was used for large farms, as well as for

the palatial residences of the *jagirdars* and maharajahs.

The special beauty of the Shekhavati great houses is their frescoes. Across their façades, on either side of the main entrance, you will see processions of elephants, dromedaries, horses and coaches. On later examples, dating from the end of the 19th century, these motifs give way to more modern forms of transport – cars, bicycles and trains . . . In the courtyards, the painted friezes depict maharajahs and maharanis, or mythological scenes from the two great Indian epics, the *Ramayana* and the *Mahabharata*, with exploits of the gods Rama and Krishna or episodes from famous folk tales, all told in cartoon form.

The Shekhavati merchants grew rich so quickly that they moved out of their newly built *havelis* as soon as they were finished. They made, instead, for Calcutta and Bombay, cities which were then rapidly expanding. The merchants still live there, returning to their villages only for special occasions – such as the ceremonies celebrating the birth of a son.

Together with the Parsees (Iranians of the Zoroastrian faith who were expelled from their country by the Muslims), these wealthy merchants, who are known as *banias*, form the dominant industrial and commercial class. The wealthiest of them all are the Birla family, whose financial interests include the manufacture of the Ambassador, India's national car. They, too, originally came from Shekhavati.

Today, fabulous villages such as Mukangarh, Laxmangarh, Nawalgarh, Dundlod, Fatehpur and Madawa are virtually ghost settlements. The *havelis* are uninhabited except by guardians and the odd tenant or squatter. The rooms are silent and unused. But the paintings remain, as witnesses of a glorious past.

There is another architectural curiosity found only in Gujarat – the *baolis*. These are underground palaces with their rooms arranged around wells – clearly designed for the hottest months of the year, May and June, when the heat reaches suffocating levels and the wait for the monsoon seems unending.

Tea and spices

The first contact a foreign visitor makes with the Indian countryside is often the strange little townships of concrete shacks that cluster around rural crossroads. These have sprung up with the development of motor transport and are unrelieved eyesores; but if you can overcome your disappointment at not finding yourself in an unspoilt village, you will be rewarded with a fascinating glimpse of Indian life. As stopping places for buses and lorries, they are filled with travellers of every kind. The favourite roadside halts are the tea stalls – an institution common throughout Northern India – which serve not only tea but often light meals and snacks as well.

Although the tea plant is native to India, the first commercial plantations were set up by the British in 1834 with plants imported from China. The Indians soon developed their own recipe for the drink, boiling up the leaves in a pan with sugar, water and plenty of milk, often adding cardamom and cinnamon to spice up

the taste, and then serving it in cups or glasses, strained and piping hot.

Food at the tea stalls varies. There may be a big pot full of cauliflower or potato curry, perhaps a few pieces of curried chicken or lamb. These come with rice, *chapatis* or *parathas* (*chapatis* are cooked dry, *parathas* in oil or butter), or sometimes with *puris* – dough balls dropped into boiling oil where they puff up and then collapse like punctured footballs on the plate.

Snacks include *pakoras*, a kind of vegetable doughnut which is made with peppers, onions or potatoes dipped in batter then plunged into hot oil; fried fresh noodles; and *samosas*, triangular envelopes of pastry filled with spiced meat or potato. Whatever the savoury snack or *namkin*, it comes liberally sprinkled with hot cayenne pepper.

Next to the tea stall there is invariably a tobacconist, sitting cross-legged all day in his narrow kiosk, selling

Every small town has its tailors, their open-fronted workshops in rows along the street. You buy your piece of cloth a few shops away and take it to be made up immediately into a skirt or blouse.

the tiny Indian cigarettes known as *bidis*. These are tight little rolls of tobacco leaves fastened with a delicate thread, which give off a sweet smell strongly reminiscent of autumn bonfires.

The tobacconist also sells betel leaves, which he keeps in a pile on his counter and sprinkles with water from time to time to keep them fresh. The leaves, which come from the betel pepper (a separate plant from the betelnut or areca palm) are about four inches long and a soft green colour. Like coca in the Andes or *qat* in the Yemen, betel leaves are chewed slowly. They stain the saliva red and contain mildly stimulating alkaloids. They are said to be good for the digestion, but recent medical studies have linked them with mouth cancer. For added flavour, each customer will ask for an individual preparation of his or her own: a sliver of cabbage, a dash of cardamom or turmeric and a piece of perfumed betelnut, all rolled up into the leaf.

For the more elaborate dishes in Indian cuisine, you must eat in a family home. The meal there is likely to be very different from what we are used to in Indian restaurants or from supermarkets in Britain.

Dress sense

Although the pattern is slowly changing, women in India tend even now to be more conservative than men, both in manner and dress. In the big cities, where men often greet each other with a Western-style handshake, women rarely touch strangers, especially men. The traditional greeting or *namaste* – palms together and pointing upwards as if in prayer – remains the norm. Similarly, city men have taken to wearing jackets and ties, while women are seen only rarely in trousers and, with the exception of Rajasthan, almost never in skirts or dresses. In the countryside, men wear loose trousers made of light cotton – *payjama* (hence our word 'pyjamas') – and a long collarless shirt known as a

Dentists, who are often Sikhs (recognisable by their beards and turbans), work out in the open. They spread a cloth on the ground and lay out a set of instruments. They are basically tooth-pullers of the crudest kind, who know nothing of anaesthetics or disinfectants. Anyone who has toothache just squats down and submits.

Here, on the River Yamuna in Agra, a laundress has just finished her work. She beats the clothes with the long wooden beater by her left foot, which means that the buttons often get knocked off. Because of the dirt that sometimes soils the clothing, the washers, or dhobis, are considered impure. Along with the tanners, street sweepers and others, they are classed as Untouchables.

Outside the period of the great fair, which takes place during the full moon in the month of Kartik (around November), Pushkar is just a large village. It does not have enough houses to accommodate the tens of thousands of people who come for the fair, so the only solution is to camp. Even outdoors, tradition is maintained. The women gather around the fire while the men attend to their trading. Rajasthani women do not wear a true veil, like the Muslims, but cover their heads with a piece of cloth which they can pull down over their faces.

kurta. Women in both town and country continue to wear saris.

The sari is more than a mere piece of clothing: it is a symbol, an institution. It consists of a piece of cloth with standard dimensions of five yards long by a yard wide. There is no question of a well-cut or badly cut sari, for the character of a sari depends entirely on its colours and patterns; these alone determine whether it is sober or gay, elegant, frowsy or spectacular. Some are thin and chiffon-like, others heavy with lamé or brocade. The way in which the sari is tied varies from region to region.

Women wear an underskirt under the sari, with a sort of short bodice over the shoulders and breasts, buttoned at the back and leaving the stomach bare. When a woman puts on her sari she tucks one corner of the fabric into the underskirt, then gives the sari one and a half turns round her hips so that it passes just below her navel. She then makes six or seven hand-width pleats and tucks them into the underskirt again. After a final turn around the waist, the remainder is folded and slung over one shoulder.

No pins, hooks or buttons are required. The sari remains perfectly in place all day, thanks to the extraordinary grace and fluidity of the woman's movements – not, incidentally, something that 'comes naturally' to Indian girls, but the product of long and patient training. Young girls practise with half-length saris that go just once around the waist then over the shoulder, while their mothers watch their progress with a keen, critical eye.

Castes and maharajahs

Some 82 per cent of Indians are Hindus, but even the remaining 18 per cent – Buddhists, Sikhs, Muslims and Christians – have all been influenced by the hierarchical Hindu social system which divides Indians into separate strata and castes.

The caste system is an organic part of the Hindu religion and its doctrine of reincarnation. People who lead virtuous lives are born again into a higher caste, perhaps as a priest or a king, while people who lead wicked lives can expect to be demoted at their next birth, returning as Untouchables.

Society is divided into four major strata (*varnas*):

priests and intellectuals, kings and warriors, peasants and craftsmen, and workers. The Untouchables, also known as *parias*, are placed below the lowest *varna* – and are not in fact considered to be part of the system at all. They take the dirtiest and most unpleasant jobs – collecting rubbish, cleaning lavatories, tanning leather, and anything to do with excrement and death.

Certain tribes outside the Hindu social system are associated with the Untouchables, such as the Grassias and the Bhils who have their own special costumes, manners and way of life. Both of these are visibly different from other Hindus. Other tribes, such as the Minas and Rabaris, who look and live exactly like

How to wear a sari. First put on an underskirt and a bodice, leaving the abdomen bare. Place the corner of the sari in the waistband of the skirt near the right hip (1), then go right round the waist (2 and 3). Next make six or seven pleats and tuck them into the top of the underskirt (4). Finally, drape the rest over the left shoulder.

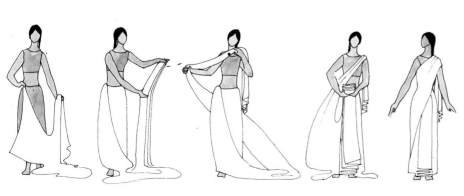

1   2   3   4   5

A woman from Jodhpur in Rajasthan carries cloth dried in the sun. After dyeing, the cloth has to be washed carefully, then laid out on the ground in long bands of vivid colours: reds, blues and yellows. The cloths are kept flat with large stones.

India, land of harmony . . . The colour and hang of these saris marry admirably with the architecture. Here, two women, whose saris show they belong to the urban middle classes, descend some steps in a town in Rajasthan.

ordinary Hindu peasants, are still regarded as highwaymen and thieves because this was the usual occupation of their forebears.

Some tribes simply prefer to stay outside the system. One example is the Gadolia Lohars, dark-skinned wandering tinkers whose prettily carved carts can be seen moving from village to village as they ply their trade of making and mending tools. Some ethnologists believe them to be the ancestors of European gypsies, pointing to the similarity in trade and to their refusal to conform to the rules of society. According to their own

legends, the Gadolia Lohars were once Rajput vassals of the Maharajah of Chittor (ancient capital of the kingdom of Udaipur), who, after being defeated by the Muslims, swore to renounce all the comforts of a settled life until he got his revenge. A group of faithful warriors shared his vow and have been wandering ever since.

The castes (*jatis*) are categories within the different *varnas*. A person's caste determines what he or she can eat and whom they can marry. There are several castes of warriors who are not allowed to intermarry, such as the Marathas of the Bombay region and the Rajputs of Rajasthan. The story goes that an 18th-century leader of the Marathas, Sivaji, who later became a hero for his military successes against the British, once took a meal with one of the grandest of all the Rajput leaders, the Maharajah of Jaipur. This was unheard of, the Rajputs being considered superior to the Marathas, and a shared meal implying a certain equality of status. The event

In a house in Mandawar, in Shekhawati, a woman makes butter by churning the milk with a rod rotated by a length of cord.

A potter in a village in Maharashtra demonstrates an ancient technique. By adding clay as she goes along, she builds up this large urn bit by bit. Potter's wheels are more commonly used, but even then hand-shaping comes into play.

caused such a sensation that it is talked of to this day.

The warrior castes are particularly interesting, providing case-studies for historians, sociologists and ethnographers. The feudal mentality continues to exist in many parts of India, and maharajahs and *jagirdars* still retain much of their former prestige. All the leading families can trace their origins back to mythical times, and there is a special caste, the *charans*, whose traditional occupation is to sing and narrate the genealogies and ancestral exploits of local potentates.

There are thousands of such legends. One example is the legend of Bikaner, which comes in two parts. It opens with the death of the nephew of a goddess, Karni Devi, who prays to Yama, the God of Death, begging him to bring her nephew back to life. Yama refuses, saying that the boy's soul still has to go through millions of reincarnations and that he has no power to permit short cuts. The goddess takes this badly and swears that not a single soul from her family will go to Yama. They will all, instead, live in her temple in the form of rats. This explains the extraordinary spectacle of the temple of Deshnoke, ten miles from Bikaner, where thousands of sacred rats throng the courtyard – a bizarre and unforgettable sight. The rats are protected from birds of prey by a metal grille, and anyone who kills one, for whatever reason, must offer a solid silver replica of the rat to the temple to expiate his crime.

In the second part of the legend, Karni Devi's brother, who is the *jagirdar* of a small village, takes a trip to Afghanistan. He is captured by Muslims and risks missing his daughter's marriage to Rao Bika. Karni Devi turns herself into an eagle, swoops down to the prison to rescue her brother and carries him off home just in time for the festivities. Rao Bika then founds the town that bears his name, and the eagle remains to this day the symbol of the royal house of Bikaner.

The farther down the social scale, the greater the number of castes. The *jatis* are similar to the guilds of medieval Europe, although there are important differences. A potter who changes trade and becomes a labourer, for example, remains a potter by caste. Often you will find that out of a similar-looking group of peasants one turns out to be from the *bhat* caste (puppeteers), another from the *lohars* (blacksmiths), and another from, say, the bracelet-makers. However much economic roles may change, social rank, and the mentality that goes with it, remains the same.

Several taboos, particularly food taboos, form barriers between the castes, although the rules of marriage are the strictest and most impenetrable barrier of all, even between sub-castes. A really Westernised family might permit a son or daughter to marry outside their sub-caste, but very rarely outside the caste itself.

Most marriages are arranged. The two families are brought together by a marriage broker and decide on the match, often without consulting their children. Horoscopes are exchanged and a propitious date for the wedding is calculated. The dowry is then agreed; paid by the bride's family among Hindus, and by the groom's among the Muslims, it can place a heavy burden on a family. The bridegroom is entertained by his future parents-in-law. On the day of the wedding, a costly and elaborate affair, the groom rides up on horseback, with a small boy sitting behind him to bring him luck and many sons. Continuance of the male line and the family name is regarded as important.

In certain villages, after the wedding ceremony the groom must touch a symbolic wooden grille known as a *toran* with a sword or branch before the bride can enter her new home. When she does go in, she must do so without touching the threshold.

A people of sculptors and painters

Jaipur, capital of Rajasthan, is a centre of Indian arts and crafts. A whole district is occupied by sculptors' and painters' workshops, where the sound of chisels on stone rings throughout the day. Here you can watch a

The potter's wheel is mounted on a small wooden cone and is driven by a stick that fits into a hole in its surface. The potter has to set the wheel spinning fast enough to give himself the time to produce his pot.

Hammered brass bowls of all sizes are used for storing water and cereals. The bottoms and sides are soldered or riveted together. Smiths also make smaller pieces: brass plates and containers for food and animal fodder.

The China tree or Persian lilac is one of the most common trees in India. It is associated with the goddess Parvati and, because of this, has the reputation of being able to cure smallpox. Its leaves and fruit are also used to make a number of medicines, and country people brush their teeth with its twigs. The China tree is also a bringer of good luck. A girl will sometimes receive a stranger with a spray of it in a pot on her head.

The basic structure of this house is extremely simple: branches lashed together with cord and covered with a layer of dried mud. On top is a sprinkling of thatch by way of a roof.

great block of white marble from quarries nearby turn into a statue of Shiva, or Durga, protectress of the Rajputs, or the mythical ancestor of a dynasty of merchants or warriors.

There is something magical in these sculptors' workshops. Vividly painted stone gods and goddesses, and the heroes and heroines of legend, stand about like actors in the wings of a theatre, waiting to go on stage. For the passer-by they make a useful lesson in Indian mythology. There is Ganesha the elephant-headed god, the remover of obstacles and patron of learning, the pot-bellied scribe of the epic of the *Mahabharata* and the son of Shiva, who is often found in temple doorways. Next to him may be Vishnu, protector of the world, supported by the coils of the divine serpent Sheshnag; or Shiva, like Vishnu, one of the supreme Hindu gods, mounted on a bull, with his wife Durga riding on a lioness nearby . . . The figures are sculpted to order for family altars or temple sanctuaries: the living past of India fashioned in stone.

Painters in Northern India have long specialised in exquisite miniatures. The technique can be seen in ancient Hindu, Buddhist and Jain manuscripts which predate the Moghul paintings by centuries. It still thrives today. The painters work on canvas, paper, cloth, bone, horn or ivory – usually in *gouache* (water-colour mixed with gum). Their themes and methods have hardly changed over hundreds of years. Favourite subjects include Padmini, the queen who threw herself into a fire with all her followers to avoid falling into the clutches of the Muslim invaders; the lovely but despotic empress Nur Jahan, wife of the Moghul emperor Jahangir; and Mumtaz Mahal, wife of Shah Jahan, who built the Taj Mahal in her memory. Images of court life are a speciality – as are animals, often sensitively

portrayed. Such scenes as warriors on horseback, maharajahs on elephants, camels carrying treasure, or gazelles and lions in the forest often contain superb animal portraits.

The continuing vitality of miniature painting and marble sculpture in modern India is remarkable. Unfortunately, other art forms are in decline. One of these is sculpture in wood, which now thrives only in Gujarat. Wood-carving of a more humble kind, though, is found everywhere, from the decorative door lintels that adorn the homes of the rich to the little wooden

Turmeric is a root frequently used in Indian cooking; it is ground with a heavy stone grinder rotated by a wooden handle.

In the village of Osian, near Jodhpur, an old man sieves grain; after threshing and winnowing, this is the final operation in the separation of the grain from the chaff.

animals sold in the street markets of Benares as children's toys.

While Westerners think of handmade objects as luxuries or souvenirs, in India many everyday things are still made by hand – tables, boxes and toys – as well as more ornamental items such as chessmen, statuettes, cigarette holders and pillboxes. These are often made of woods, such as sandal and teak, or of more precious materials, such as ivory and horn.

Near Jaipur lies the village of Sanganer, where handmade paper is still made. Old newspapers, notebooks and magazines are pulped, then hand-rolled and screened to make individual sheets. Before the arrival of the European colonial powers in India, this was the only kind of paper available. It is now disappearing fast.

Goldsmiths, jewellers and metalworkers

The variety of jewellery in India is endless. Not content with what Westerners might consider the usual places to hang necklaces, pendants, earrings, bracelets, rings and brooches, girls pierce their noses too. Once they are married, they may add rings on their toes and ankles, preferably in silver, but even tin will do. Some of this jewellery can be extremely heavy – massive ankle and neck-rings, for instance, often trailing dozens of filigree pendants, or chains of supple silver mail. Such heavyweight ornament is not cheap. A family's entire fortune may be tied up in a woman's jewellery, Indians often preferring their money in this tangible form to the paper wealth of bonds, share certificates and deposit accounts at the bank.

Precious stones are not such a feature of popular jewellery as they are in the West, although Jaipur does a brisk trade in them, particularly rubies. Craftsmen work the stones on an abrasive wheel, first cutting and then polishing the facets. This technique gives relatively crude results so that, despite their exceptional purity, Indian rubies are lacking in brilliance. Precious stones are bought largely by city people and foreign tourists. Peasants prefer opaque materials such as metal, agate and ivory. Agate (a form of veined quartz) is collected from riverbeds, heated, cut and polished. It is used in bracelets, necklaces and earrings, but also in the manufacture of domestic objects such as trays and bowls. The finest ivory – taken from the central core of the tusk – is hard and virtually imperishable. It is reserved for carving small statues and figurines. The outer part of the tusk is cut into rings and made into exquisite bracelets which the women of Gujarat, Rajasthan and Bihar wear in multiple sets like sleeves over the full length of their arms. Alternatively, dyed red and ornamented with gold, ivory bracelets make handsome engagement presents for young couples, traditionally given by the uncles of the family.

Strollers in the Tibetan market in Delhi – so called after the Tibetans who run the stalls rather than the products they sell – will notice the quantities of copper and brass objects for sale: trays and pots of every kind, kitchen utensils, pie dishes, bowls, casseroles, cups, pitchers for carrying water, whether sacred water from the Ganges or plain water from the well, ashtrays, jugs and so on. There are even brass toys – little chariots pulled by elephants, horses and buffaloes – which are made for children in the villages of Madhya Pradesh. At the luxury end of the market there are the *bidri*, copper and brass objects beautifully inlaid with silver. These are a product of Aurangabad in Maharashtra, where they also make the finest filigree jewellery.

The Korean squirrel is common throughout Northern India, where its habitats include the beautiful parks of New Delhi; the animal is used to human beings and will even eat from their hands. Legend has it that Vishnu once caressed one of these graceful creatures and left the trace of his fingers in the white markings on its back.

Camels form the main item of trade at the Pushkar fair. They are well adapted to life in the Thar desert, in the west of Rajasthan, where they transport goods and draw water from the wells. Their owners wear the Rajasthan turban, which is different from the Sikh version in that it can be put on and taken off like a hat.

Counting money after a day's trading at the animal fair at Pushkar.

Inlays of precious stone

When, in the year 1631, the empress Mumtaz Mahal died, her husband Shah Jahan could not overcome his grief. He decided to build a mausoleum worthy of his beloved, and summoned architects from all over India, Persia and Central Asia. The result of their work was the Taj Mahal, six miles from the centre of Agra on the bank of the River Jumna, the most famous building in India and one of the most beautiful in the world.

The awestruck accounts of travellers ever since have borne witness to its perfection of form. One such was Major-General W.H. Sleeman, whose *Rambles and Recollections of an Indian Official* describes his first visit there on New Year's Day 1836:

'We had ordered our tents to be pitched in the gardens of this splendid mausoleum and we reached them at about eight o'clock. I went over the whole

These women are no ordinary Rajasthani peasants: they belong to one of the country's many nomadic tribes. Their arms are covered with ivory bracelets, made from the outer part of the elephant's tusks, the higher quality core being reserved for sculpture. Ivory was once imported in great quantities from East Africa by the British. Bracelets like these are not considered a sign of particular wealth.

The richness of Rajasthani jewellery is remarkable. Brooches, necklaces, heavy bracelets, rings, nose-rings and earrings are worn in great profusion; and it is not uncommon for a whole family's fortune to come in this portable form.

building before I entered my tent, and, from the first sight of the dome and minarets on the distant horizon to the last glance back from my tent-ropes to the magnificent gateway that forms the entrance from our camp to the quadrangle in which they stand, I can truly say that everything surpassed my expectations . . . After going repeatedly over every part, and examining the tout ensemble from all possible positions, and in all possible lights, from that of the full moon at midnight in a cloudless sky to that of the noonday sun, the mind seemed to repose in the calm persuasion that there was an entire harmony of parts, a faultless congregation of architectural beauties, on which it could dwell forever without fatigue . . .

'I asked my wife, when she had gone over it, what she thought of the building. "I cannot," said she, "tell you what I think, for I know not how to criticise such a building, but I can tell you what I feel. I would die tomorrow to have such another over me." '

Among the Taj Mahal's many marks of workmanship and design are its panels of marble inlaid with fine and precious stones. This type of inlay, on black or white marble, has been made in Agra since the 17th century. Boxes for pills, cigars and cigarettes, plates, trays, chequerboards, vases, perfume bottles and other domestic and ornamental items are made from it. The precious stones are sanded down to a flat surface, then set into hollows cut from the marble.

Floral patterns occur most often, with leaves in green malachite or Indian jade, and petals in pink, brown or purple agate, lapis lazuli (royal blue or ultramarine), or mother-of-pearl. Lesser-known minerals provide the craftsman with a full palette of colours, which he will use to show the striations of a petal or the veins in a leaf, with a subtlety of tone that rivals the delicacy of painting.

Silks and tapestries

Textiles are another Indian speciality. Their silks, cottons, wools and linens, whether plain, patterned or coloured and whatever their use – for clothing or soft furnishing – are second to none in the world.

Surat, in Gujarat, specialises in the production of gold and silver thread. Two types are made: the real thing, made of authentic precious metals; and a stunning version of the real thing. You find Surat thread in the most luxurious clothes, either woven into the fabric or added as embroidery. Shawls, turbans, hats and saris are often given an extra sparkle by its presence.

In Agra craftsmen take this luxury a stage further, making elegant handbags for uppercrust Delhi and Bombay wives from plaited silver and gold threads, with agates worked into the material. The price, considering the cost of the materials and workmanship, is remarkably low. The variety of cloths is staggering: from simple industrial cottons to shimmering silks and satins, and from muslins to misty chiffons. Patterns and colours vary greatly across the country, as you soon discover if you visit local bazaars.

Some of the woven cloths look as if they are prints, so rich and elaborate is the design, but a closer

inspection reveals that the pattern is made up of single-coloured threads. For the weaver this means a laborious series of changes in the colour of the thread in the shuttle. Patan, in Gujarat, specialises in this type of weaving, but you will also find it in Bhutan and among the tribes near the Burmese frontier. Its most perfect form, however, is in the figured damasks and brocades of Benares. The threads of the weft (running side to side) are hidden behind the warp-threads (running top to bottom) for given lengths; they then emerge to create a raised pattern on the cloth. This allows some impressive effects. Often a central image – say a court or hunting scene, or an arrangement of fruit or flowers – stands out

Muslims account for about 10 percent of the population of India – or more than 80 million people. Even though the majority of Indians are Hindu, India remains one of the most important Muslim countries in the world. The women wear different costumes according to their regions, but most are veiled.

from a field of gold. Not surprisingly, such cloth is expensive, even though producing it is made easier by the perforated-card system which was invented by Jacquard in the early 19th century. The brocades go to make up the most elaborate saris, and are also used for wall hangings.

There are no factories and few workshops in the Benares textile industry. Most of the cloth is woven by women working at home. They use thread provided by the trading companies, who send round their agents to pick up and pay for the finished work. The system provides a useful supplement to many a hard-pressed family's income.

Built by the Maharajah Jai Singh, a lover of fine architecture, town planning and astronomy, the Palace of the Winds at Jaipur is one of the most celebrated monuments in Rajasthan. The stone screens in the windows were designed to permit the Maharajah's wives to watch feasts and processions without being seen.

In Sanganer a simpler and cheaper method is used. Lengths of cotton are laid out over large tables, and designs printed on them using carved wooden blocks. These are 'registered' or lined up along a wooden frame. The motifs include animals, flowers and geometric figures, and the printed cloths go to make bedspreads, wall hangings and cushion covers. Since it is cheaper for the manufacturers to produce new colours than new wood blocks, the same design is repeated year after year in the markets at Jaipur, only in different colours.

Another interesting technique is knot-dyeing. A piece of chiffon (which is particularly well suited to the process) is dyed a light colour, then hundreds of little knots are made all over the surface and tied with pieces of thread. The knotted chiffon is dipped again, but in a darker dye. The material is dried and the knots undone, leaving a pattern of tiny pale circles on a dark background. This method is used all over the western part of the Northern plain, as well as in remoter areas such as Ladakh, where the technique is cruder.

The Indians make marvellous embroideries in a tradition handed down from mother to daughter over centuries. Wall hangings, cushions, tablecloths, waistcoats and skirts are embroidered with images of girls, flowers, elephants, fruits, often in the most startling combinations of colours: rows of green flowers on a mauve background, or strawberry-pink gazelles against ultramarine blue. Indian women adore bright colours and are not afraid to use them boldly. Blue and red – and all the shades in between, from mauve to claret – tend to dominate. The embroidery will often cover the entire cloth, which glints with tiny sequins scattered across its surface like stars.

Temples of Wonder

Khajuraho, an arid no-man's-land towards the Uttar Pradesh border, is the remote setting for one of India's most magnificent attractions – nearly two dozen ancient temples, all of which were built between AD 950 and 1050, before the onslaught of Islam. Their inaccessibility meant that these extraordinary temples largely survived desecration at the hands of ravaging Moslem hoards.

Built of sandstone, the temples are elaborate, towering structures built on terraces facing the east. Their design is strict, following a maze-like layout which surrounds a central core room, the *garbhagriha,* where the image of the god to whom the temple is dedicated is housed. This inner sanctum is enclosed within a central tower or *sikhara.* The entire building is decorated with masterly sculpture friezes. These invariably depict the gods and goddesses, animals and customs of Indian mythology. Seductive 'apsaras', or nymphs from paradise, cavort and pose provocatively with exotic hybrid beasts .

Probably the most impressive of the temples is Kandariya Mahadev. With a huge spire, some 33 yards high, and a perfectly preserved central shrine, it dwarfs the other temples around it and contains an extraordinary collection of over 870 separate statues, all exquisite in their individuality.

The Southern States

Just two hours by air from Delhi, Madras is the gateway to a different world: the south of India. This is Dravidian India, its history uninterrupted at first by the Aryan invasions that spilled into the North some 4000 years ago. The Dravidians are dark-skinned and speak languages whose origins have nothing in common with the Indo-European tongues of the North. They have lived in Southern India ever since prehistoric times.

A feeling of change comes over you the moment you set foot in one of the four Dravidian states: Tamil Nadu, Kerala, Karnataka, Andhra Pradesh. Yet there is something else too: a divide in the more recent history of India that has sharpened the contrast between North and South. The conquest by the Muslims in the 12th century of the Indo-Gangetic plain from the Punjab to Bengal brought Persian and Arabic influences to the culture of Northern India: from architecture to women's clothing, and from music to patterns of thought. The South remained almost completely Hindu.

Dravidian culture – as well as its languages and peoples – is one of the great survivals of the ancient world. Religion plays a great part in daily life. The temples are like gigantic story-books, their frescoes and sculptures illustrating the myths and legends that haunt the minds of the people. Inside, the temple is a mass of people, praying, adoring, prostrating themselves before their divine images, but also hurrying about, chatting, laughing and shouting. For religion and life dissolve into one.

To speak of 'Dravidian culture' as a homogeneous entity is misleading. More than 200 million people live in the four main South Indian states: in Tamil Nadu they speak Tamil; in Kerala, Malayalam; in Karnataka, Kannara; and in Andhra Pradesh, Telugu. Each language has its own alphabet and literature.

A fifth territory, measuring about 60 miles by 40 miles, is neither Hindu nor Dravidian: 40 per cent of the inhabitants are Christians and speak Konkani, a dialect of the Maharashtra and Karnataka coasts. This is the former Portuguese colony of Goa, which was reunited with 'mother India' in 1961. Four and a half centuries of colonial rule have left a deep impression, both physically – in the white churches and bell-towers that stand sentinel over hillsides and village rooftops – and culturally, in the customs and thought of the people. When you take your seat at a café table in the capital, Panaji, and see native girls walking past in miniskirts, you may well begin to feel that you have been blown ashore in some secret pocket of the Mediterranean.

A chequerboard of cultures

Leaving Madras, the capital of Tamil Nadu, and travelling south by the coast road, you skirt miles of lovely beaches fringed with palm and casuarina trees. Apart from a few fishing villages, the coast is sparsely populated, since the Tamils are farmers rather than mariners by inclination. An hour's journey brings you to Mahabalipuram and its magnificent temples, then to Pondicherry, which was ruled by France from 1816 to 1954 and where the policemen still sport gendarme-style uniforms. The town is best known now for its *ashram* (religious centre) founded by Sri Aurobindo (1872-1950), a mystical philosopher who took refuge here in 1910, after spending two years in prison under the British for his anti-colonial activities and writings.

Apart from the *ashram*, which continues to flourish with a worldwide following, there is little else to detain the visitor in Pondicherry. The best route from here

Rice seedlings are transplanted from their beds to flooded fields or paddies where they grow to maturity. Replanting the rice is a long and laborious operation, which makes rice a luxury cereal compared with sorghum or millet.

turns inland, to the rice paddies and Tamil villages that chequer the fertile, well-watered countryside in a pattern that has scarcely changed in thousands of years.

Rice (a member of the grass family) is thought to have been first cultivated in India some 5000 years ago. The seeds are sown in soil, then, when the seedlings are between three and seven weeks old, they are transplanted to paddy fields flooded to a depth of about four inches where they grow to maturity. The rice fields of Tamil Nadu are divided into squares, each a different shade of green, depending on the stage of growth of the rice.

The coconut palm is a tree of life. It provides wood for construction, and leaves to cover the roofs of houses. Its fruit is eaten and its oil is used on the hair. The fermented sap makes palm wine, which can be distilled as toddy or arrack. Finally, the fibres covering the nut are used to make mats.

The Tamil women wear bright, even garish, saris, complemented beautifully by their dark skin. They work in long lines in the fields or walk in columns along the country roads, balancing baskets or copper pots on their heads – the most elegant of the obstacles that make driving in rural India so frustrating. Motor vehicles are continuously forced to zigzag between ox carts carrying produce to the markets, animals, men, women, children, and even sheaves of corn laid out on the roadway to be threshed by the wheels of passing traffic.

The countryside along the road from Pondicherry to Tiruchchirappalli (Trichinopoly) is studded with temples, including Chidambaram, Kumbakinam, Gangaikondacholapuram, Darasuram, and – the most impressive of them all – Thanjavur (Tanjore). Next to these Cyclopean constructions, with their towers and encircling walls, the villages seem insignificant. Yet the temples were built for the local inhabitants, rather as the Gothic cathedrals of Europe served people who lived, by and large, in hovels.

The temple complexes include bathing cisterns, gardens and alleys planted with trees, and often schools and markets as well. Their construction relies on families of architects who pass on the designs from father to son.

The Tamil Nadu plain extends southwards for 400 miles, saved from monotony by the wealth of lush greens in the vegetation, from pale yellowy lime to the darkest well-water shade. The burnt ochre patches of villages and the lurid splashes of colour in the women's saris make the background green more intense, rather as a bird's song deepens the silence around it. At the farthest point of the plain lies Cape Comorin, the apex of India's inverted triangle, and the meeting point of the Bay of Bengal and the Arabian Sea. From here you can watch the sun rise and set at opposite ends of the same horizon of sea.

North and west of Madurai the land begins to rise. The frontier between Tamil Nadu and Kerala is formed by the mountain range of the Southern Ghats, and the frontier with Karnataka by the Eastern Ghats. The word *ghat* means steps descending to water, as in the famous ritual bathing steps or *ghats* of Benares.

A few miles from Madurai the road climbs steeply to 7000 feet above sea level. Rice paddies give way to thick forest, clumps of bamboo and fields where cardamoms are grown. (This precious and highly aromatic sweet spice is one of the key ingredients of curry.) Giant bats can often be seen asleep here, when they are not being startled awake by mischievous children with bangers. There are also hordes of monkeys – animals regarded as sacred and are therefore allowed to get away with all kinds of depredations and mischief.

The forests provide valuable timber: ebony, teak, mahogany and sandalwood. Teak trees grow freely from about 2500 to 10,000 feet above sea level, with large tobacco-like leaves up to 18 inches long by 9 inches wide. The wood is prized as a building material for its durability even in hot, damp climates. Sandalwood is valued for its aromatic qualities – the wood is carved to make sweet-smelling statues of gods, rosary beads and boxes, or steamed to extract its aromatic oil, which is used in soaps, medicines, candles, incense and perfumes. Sandalwood powder is made into paste and worn by Brahmins as a forehead mark.

The forests also shelter wild animals. The large cats have been hunted close to extinction by people but you can still see herds of elephants, Asian bison and deer – even the occasional tiger or leopard if you are lucky – in the game sanctuary around Lake Periyar, where you can watch from boats or from observation huts and lodges in the park.

Periyar is in Kerala, a state that descends on a series of westward-sloping terraces to the Malabar coast. There are various levels or vegetation zones in this descent: the tea-growing zone, the coffee zone, the rubber-tree zone and the coastal plain, with its pepper vines (providing the finest black pepper in the world) and coconut palms.

The rubber tree (*Hevea Brasiliensis*) is native to South America. The first European to be aware of its existence was Christopher Columbus, who noted Indians in Haiti playing games with balls made of gum from local trees. The British introduced the plant to India, via Kew Gardens, in the late 1870s. Rubber trees thrive only in hot, wet climates within 10° of the equator. Kerala, with its tropical heat and fierce monsoon from June to August, is ideal.

The climate encourages a wealth of other vegetation too: cinnamon trees, whose dried inner bark provides the spice that was once more valuable than gold, as well as banyans, mango, banana, cashew, breadfruit and nutmeg trees, and – everywhere – coconut palms,

growing so densely that their leaves seem to form a continuous carpet when seen from the air.

The sea has eroded this coast into lagoons and inlets, with naturally formed canals connecting them. Travelling by land demands the constant use of ferries. It can be more convenient to travel by riverboat, along the route from the port of Cochin to Kottayam, Alleppey and Quilon. From Quilon a road goes to the capital, Trivandrum, and then on to Cape Comorin.

The vegetation is truly exotic, even (to a Western eye) verging on the monstrous. The banyan tree has aerial roots that dip from its branches into the earth to form new trunks. The banyan grows up to 100 feet in height and almost limitlessly outwards, so that a single tree can often look like a chaotic thicket. The jack tree (*Artocarpus integrifolia*) has large pale-green fruit about the size of a water melon, whose yellow pulp when cooked makes an excellent compote. The much smaller fruit of the mangosteen is white and juicy inside a thick brown rind. There is also the areca palm, which produces betel nuts, its long, slender trunk crowned with delicate spiked leaves; and the kapok tree, similar in shape though much bigger, which bears pods containing seeds and fibres. The fibres are used for stuffing pillows and mattresses, while the seeds make soap, cattle feed and fertiliser. Because of its water-resistance and buoyancy (it will support many times its own weight in water) kapok fibre has long been used in making lifejackets and other water-safety equipment.

Three of the most curious fruits are everyday items that we take for granted, buying them from the

The ox cart with its massive wheels is still the favourite means of transport for the peasant farmer in India. Oxen are used for both ploughing and haulage, and form an essential element in the rural economy. The flaming laburnums which line the road are common in southern India, as are other flowering trees such as the jacaranda and coral trees.

supermarket with little idea of how they come to us. Nutmeg is the kernel of an apricot-like fruit that splits open when it is fully ripe. The kernel itself is covered in a red, lacy skin which is dried and flattened to make another familiar spice, mace. The kernels are dried in the sun for six to eight weeks until the inner part shrinks away from its hard skin and rattles around inside it. The hard skin is then broken with wooden truncheons and the nutmegs taken out.

The cashew nut has an even stranger provenance. It comes from a tree brought to India from South America by Portuguese missionaries in the 15th century. The nut itself grows like a reddish-grey claw from a fruit that resembles an orange pepper (this is known as a cashew-apple and is used to make drinks and jams). The nuts have two shells, with an inflammable oil between them which gives off irritating fumes when they are roasted. Yet, despite their heavy outer defences, the nuts themselves are nutritious and delicately flavoured, and much used in local cooking.

Black peppercorns (which are, in fact, green, red or brown in nature) grow in long tresses on a climbing vine that is native to the Malabar coast. Pepper was brought overland to Europe very early on and was well known to the ancient Greeks and Romans. The peppercorns are picked when they ripen from green to red, then dropped in boiling water, which turns them black. Finally, they are dried in the sun. White pepper comes from the same peppercorns; the difference is that their outer skins are removed.

At home in Southern India

For at least half the families of Southern India home is a single room built of earth, with a roof of thatch or woven palm leaves. In one corner is a cow-dung fire, its smoke escaping through a vent in the wall just below the roof. The furniture is minimal: a mattress or two,

An ox cart, a few sheep and cows and a simple thatched hut form the basic elements of peasant life.

some rush matting, possibly a bed, a bench, and two or three chairs. There are also a few basic kitchen utensils and a couple of oil lamps – and that is all the worldly riches of an entire family. The only ornament is a free calendar issued by a business concern as a form of cheap advertising, with a garish image of a god or goddess by way of pictorial interest: Lakshmi sitting on a lotus flower, Ganesha's elephant head, or Sarasvati with a musical instrument in her hand.

Richer families have houses with more than one room, perhaps even five or six. The biggest houses have a large internal courtyard which may be paved. There is no toilet or bathroom, necessities being performed outside in the open air. Neither men nor women strip to their bare skin to wash: a man will wear his *lungi* (or *dhoti*) – a wide cloth tied at the waist and reaching to the ground – and a woman her sari. A drainage conduit carries away the dirty water, as well as the rainwater that falls on the roofs.

One room in the house is used as a shrine for family worship (*puja*), and is carefully cleaned about once a week. This task usually falls to one of the daughters of

In Kerala water is everywhere. The rivers and coastal waterways form a gigantic network of channels, and the border between sea and fresh water is difficult to establish. These channels, rivers and lagoons are all transport routes, carrying motorised water buses and these long cargo boats which are propelled by poles.

In Hindu mythology each god has his mount. Vishnu rides the eagle Garuda, and Shiva a bull. This explains the animal's sacred nature: in the villages, bulls roam freely and nobody seems to find them frightening.

the family who will be expected to dust the pictures and statues and wash the lamps and pots. Other rooms may house cows and sheep, and are swept out every day. The dung and liquid manure are collected in a large ditch and used for fertiliser. The kitchen is an area that few outsiders are allowed to enter – not because it is a female preserve, but because it is a place both of physical cleanliness and spiritual purity. The street side of the house usually has a balcony providing shade during the day and a cool place to sleep at night when the bedrooms are too hot.

As in most agricultural societies, villages in Tamil Nadu, Karnataka and Andhra Pradesh tend to be built around a source of water. The well is the traditional place for village women to meet and gossip as they fill their brass pots. In Kerala the pattern is slightly different. Water is so plentiful that each house has its own well, and the houses themselves are widely scattered, scarcely forming coherent village groupings at all. The effect is intensified by the abundance of trees, which grow so thickly that you can seldom see from one house to the next – which can make finding an address a tricky operation.

The larger houses in Kerala and Goa are built of bricks made from a porous red rock called laterite. The roofs are timber-framed, often in two stages in the pagoda style, with red tiles manufactured in the Karnatakan port of Mangalore. These houses are sometimes enormous, accommodating up to a hundred people. They are relics of a time when huge extended families used to live under one roof, a tradition that even India no longer maintains.

Holy men, or sadhus, *can be seen walking about almost naked all over India. Having renounced all pleasures and material goods, they live by begging. A* sadhu *is attached to a master* (guru) *whom he consults regularly in the course of his travels. Once he has found peace, he will retire to an ashram.*

Every house in Kerala has a well. In the other southern states of Karnataka, Tamil Nadu and Andhra Pradesh, there are usually only two wells for every village: one for Untouchables, and one for other castes.

Houses are grouped according to caste – the Brahmins near the temple, the Untouchables on the outskirts, for example. The Untouchables were until recently forbidden to enter religious buildings and even now must use separate wells to avoid polluting other people's water.

Temple life

Southern India is full of fascinating temples but perhaps the most remarkable is Srirangam – not for any particular distinction in its architecture (although it is very good), but for its sheer size and vivacity. The place is large and full of life. It has six concentric sets of square surrounding walls, with a monumental gate (*gopuram*) in the middle of each side. Twenty-four towers complete the impression of a fortress rather than a sacred building. This, at least, is how it looks as you approach it from the outside. Once inside, it is more like a bazaar, with stalls crammed in along the walls, selling cotton and silk cloths, copper pots and statuettes, perfume, books and incense. This may sound shocking to anyone brought up in the Christian tradition (we are a long way here from the discreet hush of the cathedral bookshop), but this rumbustious mixture of trade and religion seems to work perfectly well. Temples in India are not places for private contemplation and silent withdrawal from life. They are places where life goes on at full tilt.

In Kerala, the temples are slightly different, with small circular village temples crowned with conical tiled roofs. Inside, there are naive religious frescoes. Such buildings are unique in the Hindu world.

Inside, or next to, all temples there is a large tank or

Attached to a rope and pulley, a pair of oxen pull a container up from a well. Once the container reaches the top its contents are poured in to a canal. This system of irrigation is commonly practised in the South.

pool where worshippers come to purify themselves before going in to pray and make offerings. The water in these tanks is not always clean or healthy-looking; far from it. In fact, there is a distinction to be made between physical hygiene (a matter of biochemistry) and spiritual purification (symbolic actions dictated by tradition): 'clean' and 'pure' are not the same thing.

Leather and dung

Agriculture is the key to the economy, the seasons, and to daily life. There are two harvests every year: one after the winter monsoon from November to December; another after the summer monsoon from June to August. The summer monsoon is by far the wetter of the two, and allows rice to be grown. The winter monsoon serves for so-called 'dry' crops – maize, sorghum, millet, sesame, peanuts, sugar cane and rape. These plants put much less strain on the soil than rice, and allow the crops to be rotated annually. The great famines of the past no longer occur, even if harvests are threatened by irregular rainfall. Sometimes the monsoon rains simply stop after a few days, then start again a short while later; but this is enough for the sun to scorch the seedlings and make them useless. Almost as bad can be too much rain. Still, people generally have enough to eat, even if their diet is not always nutritionally as rich as it should be.

Westerners often wonder why the cow is sacred in India and its meat never eaten, a tradition which, more than any other, is regarded with bewilderment. What the Westerner dismisses as 'superstition' is based on sound business and farming sense. The cow is crucial to Indian agriculture. It is used for labouring and transport. Its milk and by-products (butter, cheese and yoghurt) are the main source of protein. Clarified butter (*ghee*) is burned in lamps and used in cooking (its great advantage over ordinary butter being that it never goes rancid). And its dung is used as both fertiliser and fuel.

The people of India use brass pots of all sizes to carry water from the wells and food to people working in the fields. The pots are washed by rubbing them with earth or with the highly acid pulp of the tamarind tree.

A cow will continue to produce all these things for many years, whereas its meat could provide for a few months at most.

After the winter harvest comes the Tamil New Year Festival of Pongal, when cows are decorated with garlands of flowers and fruits and their horns brightly painted. (The paint is indelible, so you see cows with multicoloured horns in the countryside long after Pongal is over.) Cows are left to live out their natural lifespan, and their bodies are abandoned where they drop. At this point the Untouchables move in to take the hide. Being 'polluted' themselves, according to Hindu doctrine, they have no fear of being polluted by the carcass of a cow. (Interestingly, the word *paria*, meaning outcast, is derived from the Tamil word *paraiyar*, meaning drummer. Since drums were covered with the skins of dead animals, thought to pollute anyone who touched

them, drummers or *paraiyar* had to be Untouchables.) Once the hide has been removed, the carcass is left to the vultures.

It is easy to confuse cattle such as bullocks or oxen with buffaloes. The Indian buffalo (or water buffalo) has a grey, long-haired coat and horns that run parallel to its back. It enjoys wallowing in mud, and is often found among the rice paddies where it is used as a draught animal. The bullock, by contrast, is a creature of the dry land. Each, therefore, has its uses.

A Western visitor strolling around a village may find the pervasive smell of manure unsettling. The stuff is everywhere – stocked in ditches for fertiliser, laid out to dry for fuel, even mixed with water and used to clean the house. The cow and its products are believed to be pure – again, like the purifying water-tanks at temples, pure is a religious rather than bacteriological term.

For the pious Hindu, nothing that comes from the cow is dirty. The walls and terraces of the houses are covered with 'cakes' of cow dung which dry in the sun. These make an excellent slow-burning fuel.

Other domestic animals may theoretically be eaten, but in practice seldom are. Most Southern Indians are vegetarian. This is partly due to religion – life is held to be sacred, whether human or animal – but also for economic and practical reasons. A sheep or goat provides a long-term supply of milk and wool if it is kept alive. Dead, its benefits become strictly short-term – and with refrigerators still a rarity, meat cannot be kept for any length of time.

Protein is supplied by lentils, nuts, aubergines and yoghurt – eaten at the end of every meal, either on its own or with rice. Fish is not much eaten or caught, except in Kerala, where you can taste such delicious preparations as prawns poached in coconut milk with fresh herbs. In Cochin you can watch a form of fishing from the shore, in which nets hung from crossbars are lowered into the water by a long pivoted pole, then hoisted up again a few seconds later. The catch is usually meagre – a few tiny fishes glittering in the sun. The emaciated figures of the fishermen suggest that they are never much more successful than this.

Trees of myth and legend

The catalogue of South Indian trees with practical uses is long and impressive: mango, breadfruit, passion fruit, guava, papaya and mangosteen among the fruit trees; rubber, teak and casuarina for industry and building; ebony, mahogany, rosewood and sandalwood for cabinet-making; as well as the valuable spice trees. With all this material around – most of it quite recently introduced by colonists for purely commercial purposes – it is easy to overlook the older native trees, which have lived here at least as long as humans, and have formed an essential part of their environment and culture. They are rich in mythological associations, just as the bay tree and vine were to the ancient Greeks, or the oak to the ancient Britons. These native trees include the tamarind, the pipal (or bo tree), the margosa, the coconut palm and the palmyra. The palmyra looks similar to its desert cousin, the date palm, but its fruit is more like that of a coconut and is used in making a special kind of sugar known as *jaggery*.

Jaggery is on sale in markets in the form of brown cones of thick molasses. It is extracted from the palmyra by a special caste, the *nadars*, who until recently earned their living entirely from this trade. Their position in the pecking order is a humble one – on the border between the *sudras* (the fourth order) and the Untouchables. Earlier this century they revolted against their status. Many had converted to Christianity to escape the caste system, only to find that they were still considered inferior. Riots and political pressure coincided with the ideas of Gandhi and Nehru for the abolition of the caste system; and the constitution of the new India guaranteed a quota of university places and administrative jobs to low castes and primitive tribes, giving the *naders* the opportunity they had been waiting for. Before long they were getting good jobs in the civil service, and finally one of their number became Prime Minister of Tamil Nadu: a sign that Indian society is not as rigid or traditional as many people think.

The pipal (or peepul) tree, *ficus religiosa*, has a special place in Buddhist legend, for it was under this tree that Buddha sat when he reached enlightenment. Buddhism, however, originated in Northern India; in the South, the pipal is associated with fertility. It is also linked with the god Ganesha – paradoxically, since he is a bachelor – and most examples have a sculpted figure of the god set up in their shade.

Ganesha's mother, Parvati, is associated with a

The palmyra should not be confused with the coconut palm. It grows profusely on the east coast, and its leaves are smaller. A sort of molasses called jaggery *is extracted from its fruit, and it is then sold in cones in the markets.* Jaggery *is made by a special caste: the* nadars.

Two peasant men protect themselves from the rain under these curious capes, which are made from straw that is woven tightly to keep out the water. They are busy transplanting the rice seedlings which can be seen behind them, tied in bundles.

Sadly, the elephant is slowly disappearing from India. Some wild examples can be found in the reserves of Periyar and Mudumalai, but in Kerala you still find them domesticated and working in the timber yards, where their fantastic strength does the work of a combination of crane and fork-lift truck.

The Indian cow has a large hump on its back, which is useful for fitting a yoke. The cow is sacred in India for sound practical as well as religious reasons. It is used for ploughing, transport and drawing water, not to mention milk and its many by-products. Because they do not eat meat, the Southern Indians eat plenty of butter and yoghurt for protein.

Each group of 15 to 20 villages has a market, which is generally held every week. Produce, which is sold or bartered, includes vegetables, cereals (sorghum, millet and rice), peppers, groundnuts and sesame. Animals too are sold.

different tree: the margosa, whose oil was used in the treatment of smallpox, a disease against which Parvati has special powers. Until 1977, when smallpox was eradicated by a worldwide United Nations programme of vaccination, Parvati's powers were often needed. Margosa twigs are also used as toothbrushes – with spectacular results. You will not see many people with such dazzling white teeth as the Southern Indians.

The name of the tamarind tree comes from the Arabic *tamr-hindi* or date of India. Its fruit bears some visual resemblance to the date, although the taste is acidic rather than sweet. It is used by the Tamils in cooking, as a laxative and also as an abrasive – in burnishing the fine brass pots and vessels that are the pride of most peasant households.

Perhaps the most thoroughly exploited tree is the coconut palm. Its trunk is used for building, its leaves for thatching roofs. The fibres are stripped off the fruit, and then dyed and woven to make coir mats. Once the fibres have been removed, the coconuts themselves provide coconut milk if picked before they are fully ripe (they dry out later), as well as the crisp white flesh known as copra which can be either eaten or crushed to make coconut oil. The oil is, in turn, used to make margarine or – a local custom – a lustrous hair-dressing. It can also be burned in lamps or made into shampoo and other cosmetics. Finally, the sap in the trunk can be extracted and fermented to produce palm wine or toddy, which can then be distilled to make *arak* or *feni*. This is the most common alcoholic drink in these parts.

Southern cuisine

Food in the South is predominantly vegetarian, and richly varied. *Dosas* are pancakes made of chickpea flour stuffed with spiced potatoes or eggs, and can be eaten at any time of day as a snack. If you want a full meal, you can go to one of the informal eating houses in the town, where you may be surprised to be given neither a plate nor a knife and fork, but only a banana leaf. This you clean with a little water and a wipe of the hand before the waiter comes and serves you from a kind of multiple mess tin. He dips in his ladle and pours a variety of stews on to the banana leaf. These are mostly mixtures of curried vegetables with *rasam*, a delicate but richly flavoured clear soup. There will also be rice *oridlis*, a kind of steamed mush of rice fragments. You can eat as much as you like for the same price, which is usually minimal, even by Indian standards. The food is eaten with the fingers, moulding the rice *oridlis* into a rough ball with the different stews, and adding mango chutney or lime pickle at will. Grated coconut or coconut milk is provided to cool down the hottest curry.

Afterwards, yoghurt is served with more rice. There is no dessert, but a cup of sugary tea or coffee provides some sweetness. Southern India grows plenty of tea but little coffee, even though the Tamils are great coffee drinkers. The coffee is served piping hot, with milk and sugar, in metal cups. If you want to cool it before drinking, you pour it into a new cup, then back again, and so on until the temperature is right.

In the higher-class restaurants, the banana leaf is replaced by metal bowls filled with the various curries, while the rice is placed at the centre of the table on a metal tray or *thali*. If you eat in a South Indian home, you will find that the males of the family eat before the women, who serve the meal and wait patiently to sit down later. It is easy to interpret this as a sign of male oppression (or luxury) but the separate roles are happily accepted. The women appear docile and submissive, but in fact are in charge of the home and play an important part in all family decisions, whether financial, practical or moral. Conflict is rare, and domestic violence practically unheard of. Most marriages are arranged and

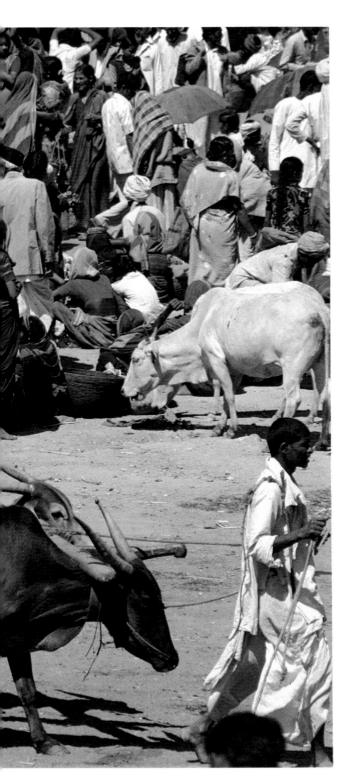

Indians love games. On slack days shopkeepers often pass the time while waiting for customers with a game of pacisi. *The pieces are made of wood, the dice of mother-of-pearl, bone or* ivory. *Chess and cards are also played, which is scarcely surprising since they were first imported to Europe from India by the Arabs.*

Fishing is a secondary activity in the south-eastern state of Tamil Nadu, but important in Kerala. The fishermen are generally poor, losing much of the value of their catch to the wholesaler.

couples who marry for love are regarded as rather odd. Love, say the Indians, comes after marriage, not before. The divorce rate, compared with Western countries, is extremely low; divorce as a social convention is hardly accepted in India.

The sacred duty of marriage

Marriage is one of the pillars of Hindu society, a sacred duty like having children. To remain single or childless is a great misfortune. Even a *sadhu* (a holy man who lives by begging) is expected to have raised a family and provided for his children's education before taking to the road.

Even the gods get married in India – the ideal couple being Shiva and Parvati. Legend has it that a demon was laying waste the earth and sky and that, according to a

This magnificent boat is typical of Kerala. It is propelled by long poles, sometimes assisted by a sail. Every year in July and August, at the feast of Onam, similar boats take part in spectacular races.

Cochin, halfway down the coast of Kerala, is the region's biggest port. Its modern docks with cranes and ocean-going ships are also the setting for primitive wooden barges such as these. This mixture of the old and the new is typical of Kerala today.

prediction, only a son of Shiva would be able to kill it. Shiva at this time was an unlikely father – a deeply spiritual young bachelor, living deep in meditation on the summit of Mount Kailash. He had no intention of getting married. The gods sent him the beautiful Parvati with instructions to seduce him. With great skill and patience, and with the aid of the god Kama, the Indian Cupid, she managed to distract him from his meditation and, despite his violent rage at being interrupted, fulfil her mission. From their union two sons were born: Ganesha, and Subrahmanya, who duly went off and killed the demon.

Every god has his or her favourite animal, which also serves as a mount. Shiva and Parvati have a bull, Subrahmanya a peacock. Subrahmanya also has the odd distinction of being represented with six heads: a reference to an alternative legend in which Parvati had six sons but hugged them so tightly that their bodies fused into one. At any rate, despite his six heads, Subrahmanya had no difficulty finding a wife – in fact two, one divine and one human. His human wife was a young girl who had been devoted to him from childhood. When the time came for her parents to find her a husband she objected, 'But I'm already married to Subrahmanya!' Then one day, as she was praying on the beach, the god that she loved so single-mindedly appeared to her in all his majesty, and took her for his second wife.

Daily life among gods and men

Madurai, a cultural centre and university town in Tamil Nadu, is famous for its temple to Minakshi – another name for Parvati. Minakshi's image stands impassively in the goddess's shrine, receiving the devotions of worshippers throughout the day, while her consort, Shiva, waits in a neighbouring room. Every night, however, Shiva visits her carried in on a palanquin by four Brahmins. A procession of priests and worshippers escort them, while musicians play the *nadeshwaram* (a type of shawm or oboe) and the *mridangam* (a drum) – instruments that are found at all the popular and religious festivals. Once the procession reaches Minakshi's sanctuary, spectators are excluded and have to imagine most of what comes next. All they can see is that once they have put down the palanquin, the priests bring forward a cylindrical object with two feet painted on it. The faithful are then given a small piece of sandalwood paste and the palanquin sets off again for the inner part of the sanctuary.

Hearing her husband coming, Parvati removes her nose ring before going to meet him. She then washes his feet with sandalwood paste and finally leads him into the nuptial chamber. Once a year they hold a great celebration of the marriage of Shiva and Parvati in Madurai. The two statues of the gods are loaded on to a wooden chariot and towed through the town by thousands of people pulling on long ropes. It is a fantastic spectacle.

Of the two sons of this divine marriage, Subrahmanya has a certain following in the South, although Ganesha, the god with the elephant's head, is a more universal favourite – so much so that he and his parents are often called the 'holy family'. In the North of India, Ganesha is believed to have two wives while in the South he remains a confirmed bachelor. Do not be misled by the fact that he is sometimes portrayed with a beautiful woman sitting on his knee; this is his mother, not a girlfriend. She is here as a kind of touchstone: any girl he sees is compared to her, for he has sworn only to marry a girl as beautiful as his mother.

A massive, sculpted wood temple-chariot is drawn through the town of Madurai on a feast day.

The girls of Tamil Nadu decorate their long black hair with jewels and flowers – usually jasmine. The heavily scented Indian jasmine is sold in garlands in the markets or around the temples.

In Madurai, Puri and elsewhere, great processions of mobile temples are the central feature of religious festivals. The temples weigh several tons and are pulled through the town by thousands of men. In Madurai the festival celebrates the marriage of Shiva and Parvati, with decorated statues of the gods placed inside the mobile temples.

Many Tamil women wear a medallion around their neck at all times with an image of the divine couple on it. Widows, on the other hand, are expected to set aside all jewellery, including the Shiva-Parvati medallion. They are also expected to shave their heads and dress in white – the colour of mourning. Other women besides widows shave their heads. For example, you sometimes find young women who have had all their hair cut off by a priest at the temple as a sacrifice to a god. This is usually made to accompany a prayer. The two worst curses for a woman are childlessness and widowhood, although the personal misfortune is compounded by a social prejudice that holds a widow responsible – in part at least – for the death of her husband.

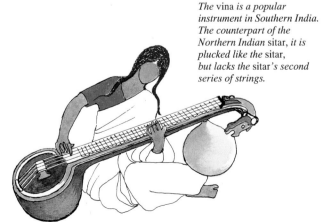

The vina *is a popular instrument in Southern India. The counterpart of the Northern Indian* sitar, *it is plucked like the* sitar, *but lacks the* sitar*'s second series of strings.*

The Toda tribe live around Ootacamund in the Nilgiri Hills, which separate Tamil Nadu from Kerala. These ancient people were probably driven from the plains towards the mountains. One of the characteristics of the Todas was polyandry, where women could take up to five husbands.

One woman, five husbands

Until quite recently, polygamy – a man having more than one wife – was legal in India. The only limitation was that the first wife had to give permission for the man to marry again. When polygamy was outlawed, existing marriages were allowed to stand, so there are still polygamous families today.

The great Indian epic of the *Mahabharata* was compiled around AD 400. It consists of almost 100,000 verses which tell the story of the struggle for supremacy between two rival families, the Kauravas and the Pandavas. The five heroes, the Pandava brothers, all share the same wife. This raises the question of how common the practice (known as polyandry) used to be in former times. Unfortunately no one knows, but evidence suggests it may have been widely accepted. The Toda tribe, living in the Nilgiri Hills near Ootacamund, have long practised fraternal polyandry, which they justify by pointing to the *Mahabharata*. Since it is probable that the Todas took to the hills originally as a result of invaders pushing them off the plains, they may well represent one of the earliest forms of Southern Indian society. A number of 19th-century anthropologists proposed that ancient India was polyandrous and matriarchal. Even today the young men in a Toda village have to pass an important test before marrying. Outside the temple door sits a heavy round stone. Only when a young man has lifted this is he considered old (and strong) enough to marry.

The human image

Dravidian sculptors have always been fascinated by the human body – whether they are casing their figures in bronze, modelling in clay, or carving them in wood, stone or ivory. Their art has been nourished by a long tradition of filling their temples with statues – there are thousands of them lining the walls. Other fine examples can be seen in the museums of Madras and Thanjavar (Tanjore). Sculptors use local materials, so you find stone sculpture in Tamil Nadu, and wood and ivory (though ivory is becoming rarer) in the states of Kerala and Karnataka.

The traditions of sculpture are maintained through schools such as the one at Mahabalipuram, an ancient port and modern tourist centre on the east coast south of Madras. Its Hindu religious complex dating from the 7th century includes caves, temples, a rock-relief depicting the 'Penance of Arjuna' (a legendary prince), and the remains of seven pagoda-like temples made of single, huge blocks of stone.

Today the student craftsmen follow ancient textbooks, learning their trade on soapstone – a soft, easily worked material which hardens when exposed to air, permitting detailed work with good durability. When they have mastered this material they move on to sandstone, and finally granite.

Physical mastery of the stone is only half the story. Since the images are devotional, representing the gods not only as static figures but dancing, moving and carrying out mythic exploits, the sculptors must also understand the meaning of their images, the philosophy behind every detail.

The gestures (*mudras*) of a carved figure are highly significant. When Shiva is represented as Nataraja, the king of dancers, for instance, he has four arms: one holding a drum, out of which the universe unfolds; another in the 'fear-not' gesture (raised right hand) to preserve the universe; another, with a tongue of fire, to reabsorb the universe into his being; and the fourth held across the chest with wrist and fingers pointing downwards.

Similarly his feet have special positions: one lifted to signify grace and release, the other on the ground to signify rest for world-weary souls, also stamping on a dwarf to symbolise the triumph over ignorance. Sometimes the sculptures carry contradictory meanings,

The houses of the Todas are roughly half-cylindrical, but viewed from the front they are actually seen to be slightly oval. The Todas are now developing and are becoming integrated into modern India. Their houses at Ootacamund have kept the traditional form, but are made of concrete.

as in the celebrated erotic sequences on the outsides of many temples, which are both a thanksgiving for the fertility and beauty of life, and a reminder to the worshipper to set aside all thoughts of the world and its pleasures as he steps into the sacred area of the temple.

Arts and crafts of the South

Other crafts also flourish in Southern India, notably textiles and jewellery. At the simplest level, cotton is used to manufacture saris, skirts for young girls, men's shirts and *dhotis* – lengths of cloth which men tie around their waists. The Banara women of Andhra Pradesh wear multicoloured striped saris which they decorate themselves with embroidery and tiny pieces of mirror – a charming practice which is also to be found among the Lambaris of northern Karnataka.

The silk-manufacturing centres of the South are Mysore and Kanchipuram. Silkworms are raised in large baskets filled with mulberry leaves. The silkworms, which are the caterpillars of Bombay moths, spin a cocoon around themselves made of one very long silk thread. This is their chrysalis stage, at which point they are killed with boiling water or steam and the silk thread carefully unravelled, each silkworm producing up to 3000 feet of thread. The silk threads are twisted together to make yarn, then dyed and woven. Unlike textile manufacture in Benares, which is organised as a cottage industry, the Mysore and Kanchipuram silk production is factory-based.

As in the North, jewellery, especially silver filigree, is made in a wide variety of places, but Hyderabad and Madurai are the best known. The Banjara and Lambani women convert all their money into jewellery, carrying their family fortunes as ornaments on their bodies. Women without money to spare wear bracelets made of glass. These are cheap and sell in a profusion of colours, and all but the very poorest can afford to buy whole armfuls, which they wear, with fine extravagance, all at the same time.

The kathakali *is the traditional dance form of Kerala; it is also a theatre of mime. Everything begins with the actors' make-up, which can take hours to apply, as their faces are completely painted over to form living masks.*

Girls of good family still study bharatanatyam, *the school of classical dance of Tamil Nadu. The rhythms, hand gestures and eye movements are all prescribed by rules which are 2000 years old.*

The dancer's hands are not painted. The fingers of the left hand are equipped with long 'nails' to help emphasise the gestures of the hands, all of which have a precise meaning. The character represented here is a 'good' prince. In the course of the story, he will probably have to fight a demon, whom he will defeat in the end.

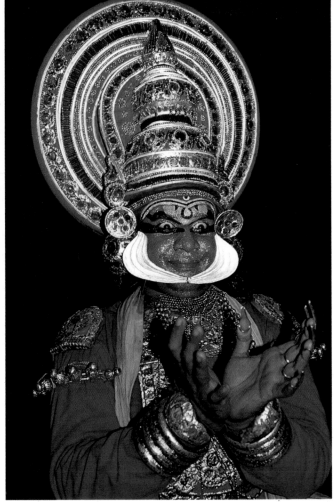

From the Golden Temple to the Roof of the World

We think of India as a triangle pointing south into the Indian Ocean, but the map reveals that it is in fact a diamond shape, with a northern as well as a southern point, reaching up into the Himalayas and Western China. This northern tip provides not only some of the most spectacular scenery in the world, but also a concentration of the four principal religions of India. The region consists of three states: Punjab, Himachal Pradesh, and Jammu and Kashmir, with populations of 17 million, 4 million and 6 million respectively.

The land rises from the plains of Rajasthan and Haryana to the summits of the Himalayas in a series of broad steps. The first is the Punjab, a rich agricultural plain of some 100,000 square miles, divided in 1947 between Pakistan and India. The eastern half, belonging to India, covers just under one-fifth of the total area. The name 'Punjab' means 'five waters', a reference to the five large rivers that water the land: the Chenab, the Ravi, the Jhelum, the Sutlej and the Indus – into which the first four flow. The plains here are fertile, the fields laid out in geometric precision and lovingly tended. The Punjab has the highest standard of living in India, providing a quarter of the country's wheat production. Sixty per cent of the population are Sikhs, with their spiritual capital in the city of Amritsar. In 1966, the southern (largely Hindu) part of Punjab was hived off into the separate state of Haryana, but even so the influential Sikh militants have continued to fight for their independence, a struggle which led to the bloody siege of the Golden Temple at Amritsar in June 1984 when more than 500 people died, and the subsequent assassination of Indira Gandhi by Sikh members of her own bodyguard.

North-east of Punjab is Himachal Pradesh (literally, 'snowy mountain state') whose capital is Simla – familiar to generations of British administrators and soldiers as the summer capital of the Raj, its social life vividly described by Rudyard Kipling in *Plain Tales from the Hills* (1888). Simla remains a charming place to visit, with its pleasant walks among wooded hills and the Himalayas hovering in the distance, although careless development is threatening large parts of the town.

As you climb towards the mountains the landscape becomes ever more attractive, the vegetation lusher and the pine woods denser. As you approach the third step up from the plains, the valley floors of Lahaul and Kashmir, you have a choice of routes: either through the Banihal tunnel, open all year from Jammu to Kashmir, or over the Rohtang Pass (13,200 feet) to Lahaul, which is open only from May to October.

Lahaul is a deep, narrow valley surrounded by high peaks, cut off from the outside world by snow for seven months of the year. It is set among breathtaking mountain slopes, glaciers, rivers and green pastures, with forts and monasteries dotted here and there. The people have a distinctive culture in which folksongs and dances enact the conflicts of gods and demons.

Kashmir (dubbed 'Paradise' by the Moghuls – and few have disagreed with them since) is roughly oval in shape and some 40 miles across at its widest point. The land is a patchwork of rice paddies, lakes, woodland and prolific orchards. The market stalls are piled high with apples, peaches, pears, cherries, plums, apricots and more exotic varieties. The woodlands present a wonderfully variegated picture, with the yews, larches, cedars, birches and pines giving subtly different shades of green.

The great Indian statesman Jawaharlal Nehru, who

Amritsar is the religious capital of the Sikhs. The Golden Temple is their holiest sanctuary. Within the temple complex is an immense pool for ritual ablutions, surrounded by a rectangular building over arcades. In the middle of the pool is the 'holy of holies', in which the sacred book of the Sikhs, the Adi Granth, *is kept.*

was Kashmiri, wrote of his Kashmir in *The Discovery of India* (1946):

'It has a hundred faces and innumerable aspects, ever changing, sometimes smiling, sometimes sad and full of sorrow. The mist would creep up from the Dal Lake and, like a transparent veil, give glimpses of what was behind. The clouds would throw out their arms to embrace a mountain-top, or stealthily like children at play. I watched this ever-changing spectacle, and sometimes the sheer loveliness of it was overpowering and I felt faint. As I gazed at it, it seemed to me dream-like and unreal, like the hopes and desires that fill us and so seldom find fulfilment. It was like the face of the beloved that one sees in a dream and that fades away on awakening.'

Ladakh, in the extreme north of India, is about as different from Kashmir as it is possible to be. Where Kashmir is rich and fertile, Ladakh is poor and arid. The reason is the Himalayas. These bar the monsoon rains which blow in from the south-west and fall so plentifully on Punjab, Himachal Pradesh and Kashmir. Kashmir has 30 inches of rain a year, Ladakh only 3 inches. The Himalayas separate the tropical monsoon climate of India from the dry continental climate of Central Asia.

Crossing this dividing wall, whether by land or air, is a dramatic experience. The 25-minute journey by air

Nimaling is a mountain pasture 13,000 feet above sea level, in the east of the Marka valley in Ladakh. A place of seasonal migration, it is inhabited for only a few months in the summer.
The animals (goats, sheep and dzhos - a cross between a cow and a yak) are penned in enclosures of drystone walls. A few people, mostly women, look after them.

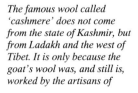

The famous wool called 'cashmere' does not come from the state of Kashmir, but from Ladakh and the west of Tibet. It is only because the goat's wool was, and still is, worked by the artisans of *Srinagar that it is universally known by the name of cashmere. The goat is bred by the Ladakhi and Tibetan nomads on the high plains of Rupshu, where the extreme cold explains its thick coat.*

Chang, *along with tea with butter, is the standard drink in Ladakh. Grains of barley are washed in a stream, then left to ferment in wooden barrels. The fermentation lasts five to seven days, after which the drink becomes sour to the taste. It can be distilled to obtain a spirit called* rakshi.

A mane *or votive structure, in one of Ladakh's typical steep-sided valleys.*

The route between Kashmir and Ladakh crosses the Dras Valley, which is inhabited by the Dards, who are Muslims of Aryan race, and therefore closer to the Kashmiris than the Ladakhis. The Dards' villages are few in number and densely built. This protects them from some of the coldest winters in the world.

The Gujar nomads winter in the plains of Punjab. They migrate slowly towards the high valleys of Kashmir at the beginning of spring with their herds of goats. Some cross the Zoji Pass and spend the summer in the Dras Valley. The men have large beards which they dye with henna; the women wear their hair in thin plaits.

from Srinagar to Leh is modestly described in one guidebook as 'one of the most spectacular short plane rides in the world'. By road – 270 zigzagging miles, impassable from late October to early May because of snow, and a two-day drive at the best of times – the journey is gruelling but magnificent, crossing the main Himalayan range at the Zoji Pass, 11,480 feet above sea level. If you are up to it physically, you can also walk it in ten days on an organised trek from Pahalgam, a hill resort in Kashmir.

The contrast between the Kashmir side of the Himalayas and the Ladakh side is brutal – from thick vegetation and carpets of wild flowers to a jagged landscape of bare rock – the dividing line a row of birch trees. Ladakh, however, has a stark beauty of its own. The rock faces vary from grey to red to ochre to

yellow, and torrents course down the steep valleys. From time to time, at the turn of a bend, a patch of green appears where water has been harnessed to irrigate meagre plots of cultivation, supporting a handful of inhabitants. Such cultivated areas occupy less than one per cent of this territory, whose surface area (45,000 square miles) is not much smaller than England.

Ladakh is a country of extremes. It is one of the highest regions in the world, with its valley floors between 10,000 and 12,000 feet above sea level. Both the highest road (the Khardong Pass, 17,650 feet) and the highest populated area on earth (the Chang-Tang plateau, 14,763 feet) are to be found here, as well as a people whose temperament, despite or because of the most arduous living conditions, is one of the most cheerful and welcoming in the world.

The Himalayan home

There is little difference between the houses in Punjab and the rest of India's northern plain. But the moment you enter Himachal Pradesh you notice a change. The houses are built of wood and decorated with door frames, window frames and balconies carved in patterns like cut-outs made from scissors and paper. Sometimes the whole front of a house is carved in geometric designs – triangles and squares, stripes, stars and friezes of all sorts. Temple architecture follows a similar pattern, with the addition of divine images of the gods.

Wood is the dominant material, both here and in Kashmir, and only the rich build stone houses. Poor houses consist of two rooms: one for the animals (where humans also sleep in winter) and the other for a kitchen. There are no windows or chimneys, and the family spend their free time sitting round a fire which serves for cooking, heating and light. The smoke from the fire hangs about in the upper parts of the room with no means of escape, while the family crouch low to avoid breathing it. The Kashmiris use only a few metal crates as tables or chairs, and feather quilts as mattresses or bed covers. The floor consists of trodden earth spread with grass which is fed to the cattle every two or three days and replaced with fresh grass.

The only light is a dim glow from the fire or an oil lamp. Parents sleep in the same room as their children, even sharing it with other couples. Partitions of cloth hung from the ceiling provide a little privacy.

In Ladakh, houses are often on three floors: the ground floor for the animals, the first for humans in winter, the second for humans in summer. Every house has a shrine-room, the *chot-kang*, on the second floor or even on the flat roof. This makes a symbolic division between the earth, with animals and the rest of the natural world, on the ground floor; the gods on the top floor nearest the sky; and people halfway between.

The ground floor is of stones bound together with earth. The walls are wider at their base than at the top for stability, but this also creates the effect of lightness and grace typical of much building in this area, most noticeably in the Potala Palace at Lhasa, capital of Tibet.

The upper floors of houses are built of bricks shaped

The hoopoe is a common bird which adapts to all kinds of climates and can be found just as often in the gardens of Delhi as in the mountains of Kashmir and Ladakh. Most of the time it walks along the grass and rummages among the bushes, looking for insects with its long beak. You rarely see it in flight.

Apart from the luxurious houseboats on Lake Dal where tourists to Srinagar stay, there is also a multitude of small native houseboats called doongas. *These usually have two rooms, with up to a dozen people living on board.*

in wooden moulds and baked in the sun. Windows are often nothing but holes, which are plugged with rags to keep out the wind and snow in winter. In Leh, the capital, glass has begun to appear, and with it wooden window frames.

Timber, though rare and costly, is essential, for without it neither roofs nor ceilings would be possible. Small rooms are roofed with parallel joists, and the

space between filled with packed twigs covered with grass and then earth. This forms the floor on the next level up. Bigger rooms such as the kitchen, where the span is too great for single joists, have one load-bearing beam across the middle, supported by a central pillar.

The kitchen is where the family gathers and where friends and relatives are received and sit chatting over a drink of *chang* or tea with butter. The Ladakhis learned

The lake people of Srinagar live in a self-enclosed social and economic world. The doongas *are moored to small islets which serve as gardens, with shacks built on them which the women use as kitchens. Travelling merchants move around on canoes and there are even floating markets. Here a man is busy tying a bundle of straw to finish thatching his roof.*

about chimneys from missionaries in the 19th century, so their kitchens are mercifully free of smoke. It seems curious that of all foreign technical innovations the Ladakhis should have chosen the chimney – especially since their way of life is so archaic in other respects. Until the arrival of cars they knew nothing of the wheel – even now they have no pulleys, wheelbarrows or even spinning wheels. Still, one can imagine the liberating effect of being able to keep warm indoors in a Himalayan winter without being suffocated by smoke . . . It saved their health too, since the Ladakhis have largely escaped tuberculosis, which sweeps through the Karakoram and the Himalayas, from Pakistan to Nepal. The hearth, which may be made of earth or iron, is placed against one wall. On one side sits the woman of the household, cooking; on the other her husband or father-in-law. Women and men sit in descending order of precedence at a series of small tables – the most senior close to the fire.

Even in this unusual costume, Sikhs are recognisable by their turbans, which serve to hide their long hair. The uncut hair is one of the five symbols of the Sikhs; the others are a short sword, a steel bangle, undershorts and a comb placed in the long hair.

Everyone sleeps in the kitchen for its warmth during the winter, and on the terrace in summer. The other rooms are used for stores, tools, food or guests.

In the Golden Temple

The variety of landscapes, economies, and ways of life to be found in these four regions is reflected in the differences of religion. The Punjab is mainly Sikh; Jammu and Himachal Pradesh Hindu; Kashmir Muslim and Ladakh Buddhist.

Hinduism, the oldest of the four, is a highly complex religion with a huge variety of deities, and dozens of different sects and traditions of worship. Its earliest sacred texts are the *Vedas*, the first known Indian

writings; these express the religious beliefs of the Aryans who invaded India between 1400 and 500 BC. An essential doctrine of Hinduism is that the human soul has to go through a series of lives (incarnations) before attaining liberation through the realisation of God. Despite the multiplicity of gods and their divine images in the temples, Hindus believe that the ultimate reality is an infinite, eternal force or being that is present in all life.

Buddhism was founded in the 5th century BC by the man now known as Buddha ('the enlightened'), although his family name was Gautama. He was a prince of the warrior caste who was so shocked by life's inevitable decline into sickness, suffering and death that he abandoned his wealth and family at the age of 29 to become a wandering ascetic and seeker of the truth. His enlightenment, revealed to him after six years of deep religious study and self-mortification, came to him finally after a night of meditation under a pipal tree. Buddha taught that suffering was the result of desire, and that the only way to overcome desire was to live and meditate according to his system, with the aim of reaching Nirvana – a state of complete understanding and release. The question of the existence of God is not addressed: the Buddha's rules of life are concerned with what happens here and now, and with what humans know for certain. Buddhism has proved a highly successful religion, spreading throughout the Far East, into Tibet, China and Japan, and South-East Asia; but numerically it is not very significant in India.

Islam came to India with the invasions from Central Asia in the early 13th century. The religion is based on

This bread (roti) *is being cooked for a great Sikh feast. The same activity can be seen at the Golden Temple at Amritsar, where volunteers cook for the thousands of pilgrims who arrive each day.*

A monastery in Leh, the capital of Ladakh. Prayers printed on cloths known as trashitaling are hung from cords and stretched out like washing across the sky.

A monk studies in the library of a monastery. The books stacked on the shelves to his left are made of long unbound sheets wrapped in cloth. The sheets are printed from wooden blocks.

the teachings of the 7th-century Arabian prophet Mohammed, enshrined in the Koran. Central to Islam are the five articles of faith – in one god, angels, the revealed books, the prophets and the day of judgement. Equally important are the five pillars of Islam: the profession of faith, daily prayer, payment of a tax to help the poor, fasting in the month of Ramadan, and the pilgrimage (or *haj*) to Mecca.

Sikhism, founded in the 15th century by Guru Nanak, takes elements from both Islam and Hinduism. Sikhs believe in reincarnation (unlike Muslims) but in only one god, who may not be represented either in pictures or divine images (unlike Hindus). Their holy book is the

Ladakhi peasant women come every day to sell vegetables in the great bazaar at Leh. There are magnificent cabbages, cauliflowers, radishes, spring onions and potatoes. Note the tall hats which are typical of the costume of Ladakhi women.

This balcony was constructed simply by allowing two series of joists to protrude outside the walls of the building. The space between them is filled in with wooden sticks, and is then covered with grass and earth.

Adi Granth, which contains hymns written by Nanak and his four successors as spiritual leaders (*Gurus*). At the end of the 17th century, the Sikhs turned to militancy under the tenth and final Guru, Gobind Singh, in response to persecution by the Mughals. It was then that they took on the surname 'Singh' (meaning Lion).

Sikhs are easily recognised by their turbans and beards; the turban hides their hair, which they leave uncut since they believe that the body must not be violated in any way. They also carry symbolic daggers for the fight against evil and a metal bracelet which reminds them of their religion every time they use their hands. Amritsar, with its famous Golden Temple, is their religious capital. The temple contains no images, only the *Adi Granth*. In a ceremony reminiscent of Hindu practices, this holy book is carried every evening on a palanquin to a separate room, where it spends the night.

The atmosphere in the Golden Temple is quite extraordinary – the word that most often comes to the mind of visitors is 'brotherhood'. Volunteers bring water to the thirsty congregation and then wash up the cups. Other volunteers cook the enormous communal meals that are served in the great refectory close to the Temple where several hundred faithful eat together. There are no priests and no hierarchy. Volunteers guard and maintain the holy places, while a democratically elected committee manages the financial and practical aspects of temple life.

Two Ladakhi women chat in a street in Leh. The piece of cloth, the lopka, *which they wear over their backs is a sign that they come from the town; country women would wear goatskin. To their right, two prayer mills are let into the wall. These are cylinders of wood or metal, or sometimes old food cans, which you turn clockwise with your right hand as you pass. Turning the cylinder causes the prayers inside to be 'recited'.*

The roof of the world

In Ladakh, 'the roof of the world', they practise a monastic form. This is the form also found in Tibet (though persecuted and discouraged by the occupying Chinese), Bhutan, Sikkim and Mustang. Tibetan Buddhism is characterised by a multitude of gods and contrasts strangely with the plain and sober humanism of the Buddha's original teaching.

The walls of the monasteries are as crowded as the Hindu temple with images of these divinities. Some have terrifying faces, with fangs, three eyes, and strings of skulls round their necks or foreheads. Others smile, radiating peace and beatitude. The frighteners are to scare away the forces of evil, the happy ones to help men forward on the way to the 'great liberation' – Nirvana.

Outside this pantheon of 'official' Tibetan divinities, the popular imagination of the Ladakhis has filled the world with legions of monsters, demons, goblins, sprites, ghosts, witches, magicians and mystical monks who fly through the air and walk on water.

There are the Tsan, red demons who are beautiful when met face to face, though lethal if you turn to look once they have passed: they have no backs, and any human rash enough to look sees lungs, intestines and a bag of inner workings so horrible that the sight of them is enough to kill him stone dead. There are witches who swoop down at night and steal the supporting beam of

Mulbekh is one of the first Buddhist villages that the traveller reaches on the road from Kashmir. The women wear headgear which is found nowhere else: a sort of cap with a long visor covered with turquoises. In other regions of Ladakh, there is another kind of hat with turquoises called a perak, *which is shaped like a cobra and covers the whole head. Some* peraks *have seven rows of turquoises and weigh more than four pounds.*

the kitchen ceiling, replace it with a strand of hair, and fly off astride their booty to sabbaths where they feast on raw meat and blood. There are the *manmo* who live high up among the flocks of ibex; these are female fairies who bring lifelong luck to any man who manages to have sex with them – provided he never breathes a word to anyone of what he has done. There are the *Balu*, goblins with sticks and large hats who become servants to anyone who can take these two things from them. The Balu are hard workers, and their masters quickly grow rich with their help – but sooner or later they steal back their hats and sticks, bringing ruin to their former masters.

The Ladakhis love these myths and folk tales, which they tell during long winter evenings when the temperature outside has plunged below zero and the family is gathered around the kitchen fire. They are passed down from generation to generation: the old people tell the stories; the young listen, enchanted.

Food and drink

Wheat, sugar cane, rice, potatoes, corn and pulses are grown in the rich plains of Punjab, fruit and rice in Kashmir. Ladakh's main crop is barley – a cereal that

On the right, leaning against the wall, is a gurgur, *a device which is used for preparing* gurgur cha, *a mixture of tea and butter. The tea is put on to boil in large cauldrons. The monk has a large brass ladle in his hand, which he uses to pour the tea into the* gurgur. *The copper jugs in the foreground are used by the young monks to distribute the drink to the adult monks during ceremonies.*

This Kashmiri ewer is used for serving kahwa, *an aromatic green tea to which cardamom and cinnamon are usually added. The Kashmiris are excellent metal workers. They work both silver and copper and even mix the two, encrusting the copper with silver to make objects called* bidri.

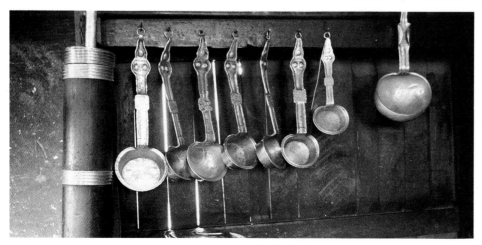

To the left, the upper part of a gurgur *is visible. It is made of wood with metal rings. Protruding from the end of the* gurgur *is a stick which is used to mix the tea and butter. The Ladakhis use a lot of ladles, usually made of copper, sometimes of aluminium. They are used for ladling water out of the pitchers where it is stored, and for serving tea or soup.*

A Ladakhi kitchen with a metal stove decorated with designs based on the lotus flower. This motif signifies that the stove is the seat of a divinity. It has a chimney, a feature common in Ladakh but rare elsewhere in the Himalayas.

grows well at high altitudes. Its grains cannot be milled into flour, however, so the Ladakhis do not make bread. Instead they cook and mash the barley, mixing it with whey, yoghurt, beer, tea or soft cheese. The mixture is called *tsampa*, and eaten with the index-finger of the right hand.

Chang is the local beer, low in alcohol and made from fermented barley. It is also distilled to make a considerably stronger drink. Tea is drunk with salt and butter and made in a big wooden churn called a *gurgur*. There are five different ways of making tea in north-west India. The way it is made in the West is the least popular. Then there is the boiled-milk and spices method, favoured in the plains, and two recipes from Kashmir: *nun cha*, reddish in colour and salted; and *kahwa*, a green, highly fragrant tea drunk with sugar, cinnamon and cardamom. Finally, there is the salted, buttered tea of Ladakh.

Potatoes and cabbages are eaten throughout all these regions, cooked in oil or curried. Spinach and other greens, known collectively as *sag* (*hag* in Kashmir, *zatsot* in Ladakh), are also much appreciated. The Kashmiris eat a lot of lamb, which is butchered in the Muslim halal tradition, and cooked in exquisite recipes such as *Rogan Josh* (with yoghurt, cream and spices), *Koftas* (meatballs) and *yakhni* (a stew with fennel seeds

and curry spices). Meat is a luxury in Ladakh, where animals are rarely eaten until they die naturally, a practice which would horrify both Hindus and Muslims. The meat is dried and eaten in small pieces in soups with greens, cheese, nettles and other vegetables.

Class distinctions

The Sikhs of the Punjab have a different caste system to the Hindu system found in neighbouring Haryana and Himachal Pradesh. The Buddhists of Ladakh and the

A woman wearing typical Kashmiri costume: no veil, but simply a scarf tied on the head; a long loose shirt and trousers. Though the Kashmiris are strict Muslims, they do not impose the veil on their women, either among the 'people of the lake', as here, or among the 'people of the land'.

Muslims of Kashmir are strictly egalitarian, although class distinctions, hierarchies and pecking orders have a way of creeping in.

Srinagar, summer capital of Jammu and Kashmir, with its gardens, river, lakes, markets and historic mosques, is a great tourist attraction. The houseboats on Lake Dal are its most celebrated feature. Yet social snobbery holds sway. The 'people of the water' (*hanjis*) are looked down upon by the 'people of the land'. The *hanjis* operate the houseboats, originally built by British traders when the local maharajah refused to let them buy land. When the British left, the houseboats were taken over by locals who now run them as tourist hotels, living themselves in houses on the islands, or on the smaller, native form of houseboat known as *doongas*. These hoteliers – waiters, boatmen, cooks, handymen and others – are regarded as social inferiors by the land-based townspeople and farmers. Marriage into their ranks is considered highly undesirable.

The people of the land think of themselves as morally superior too. They accuse the *hanjis* of being narrow-minded liars, cheats and swindlers. All this tension seethes beneath the surface of the magical water world, where shopkeepers paddle their wares around by

The shallow water and the sunny summer climate produce abundant water plants on lakes Dal and Nagir. Algae are plentiful, but the lotus, blossoming like a gem from the muddy water, is the pride of the region's inhabitants. The women collect them to use or to sell as fertiliser.

shikara – a form of gondola – laden to the gunwales with fruit, vegetables and household goods; where women pull up the lotus lilies that carpet the surface of the lake and pile them in their canoes to sell as fertiliser; where houseboats float like elongated garden sheds on a shimmering field of dark water.

According to Buddhist tradition, the only people who can be considered inferior are those whose trade is to do with killing, for Buddhists are forbidden to take life. They can eat meat, provided the animal is killed by someone else – a foreigner or inferior. Butchers, fishermen and executioners are in a lower caste than the rest of society.

In Ladakh, there are no fishermen or executioners and the butchers are all Muslims, but there is a class system of a kind. At the top sits the king, long since dethroned but still the king; followed by the nobility, similarly shorn of privileges, though they hold on to their titles; then the peasants, both rich and poor; and at the bottom of the scale, the *bedas* (acrobats and singing beggars).

Arts and crafts

Both Punjab and Kashmir are famous for their carpets. Punjabi carpets are made in small semi-mechanised factories. They are made from wool and are relatively cheap. Kashmiri carpets are a luxury item whether in wool, cotton or silk, and are made entirely by hand. They are exquisite but costly, comparable in quality to the finest Persian rugs. The making of carpets is very much a living tradition in Kashmir. Old patterns are constantly reworked to create new designs, which are then converted into the practicalities of knots, threads and colours by technical draughtsmen. The third stage in the process is when the craftsman, or team of craftsmen, turns working drawings into reality, like a musician playing from a score.

Kashmir's crafts extend well beyond carpet-making. Apart from the world-famous cashmere shawls, there is woodcarving, papier-mâché, furs, knitted goods and the *namdas*, felt wall-hangings with naive embroideries of human and animal figures in coloured threads. The wood carvings can be very small – pillboxes and pen trays – or very large: the interior of a houseboat may be covered in chiselled geometric or floral designs. The furniture on houseboats is made of carved wood, too: low tables for tea, large tables for eating, chairs, stools, settles, side tables and beds. The whole décor is often magnificently worked, creating an effect of almost unreal luxury.

Papier-mâché is something the Kashmiris are proud of. They press the paper pulp into moulds, turning out boxes, decorative eggs, vases, bowls, vanity cases and egg cups. Practically any household object can be made from this light but strong material. It is resilient enough not to break if it falls on the floor. The finished objects are painted in vivid colours with a high gloss. Flowers, birds, men and women in ancient costume shine from their surfaces like stars. The Kashmiri craftsmen no longer work to produce items of everyday use for themselves. Everything is for export or sale to visitors, whether Indian or foreign. When it comes to their own

Though not as famous as those of Iran or China, the carpets of Kashmir are among the finest in the world, whether they are silk, wool or cotton. The technique is universal. A warp is placed vertically between two large supports, while the workers - preferably children, due to the dexterity of their small hands - tie on the coloured threads of the weft following a pattern placed in front of them. The number of knots to the square inch decides the value of the carpet.

All Kashmiri artisans are men, even when the craft is weaving, embroidery or dressmaking. The designs of the embroidery are similar to those of the shawls and carpets: usually multicoloured floral motifs or palms. Sometimes the craftsman sketches in an animal or a person, ignoring Islamic convention. The work is hard, usually more than ten hours per day, for modest wages.

Three sorts of cloth are embroidered in Kashmir: wool, to make shawls; cotton, for table cloths and napkins; and felt for wall-hangings.

daily needs, the inhabitants of 'Happy Valley' prefer to buy mass-produced goods.

Once again Ladakh tells a different story. The Ladakhis make everything they need with their own hands. They shear their own animals, card and spin the wool, then weave and sew it into clothing and blankets, using combs, spindles, looms and needles that they have made themselves. They cobble their own shoes and tailor their own hats; they make their own plates, pans, jewels and tools. Even the houses that they live in are home-made.

They have strict rules for the division of labour. Women, for instance, spin sheep's wool, while men spin yak's and goat's wool. The men do the weaving and sewing. The only hint of the modern world is the use of synthetic colours, instead of natural dyes such as madder and cochineal. Otherwise everything is done in the traditional way.

Not every Ladakhi is a Jack of all trades. There are some specialists: blacksmiths, carpenters, basket-makers, shoemakers and so on. There are even craftsmen who saw up marine shells to turn into bracelets. Until recently, too, there were the *perak*-makers, the traditional art, taught by mother to daughter, of creating a female headdress in the form of a cobra. The materials were corals and turquoises brought by caravan from Mongolia. The headdresses weighed up to four pounds apiece.

The village of Chilling, tucked in between the river Zansnar and towering cliffs, has specialised for the past four centuries in the manufacture of metal goods: magnificent *chang* pots, huge copper and silver tea urns with spouts and handles in the shape of dragons, and silver teacup lids. The prices are high, especially compared to the cost of living, but the workmanship and materials are so fine that every one of these objects will last for generations.

They also make ritual objects at Chilling, particularly images of thunder (*Dorje*, a male symbol) and bells (*Tilu*, a female symbol). The main religious art in this area, however, is painting, in the form of frescoes and *tankas*.

The art of fresco painting requires faultless technique and speed of execution, since it must be done on fresh plaster before it dries, and there is no way of correcting mistakes. In the new monasteries that continue to be built in Ladakh, frescoes are still painted in the traditional style. This means that the artist has to stick very closely to the rules of Buddhist painting, with little room for personal fantasy or free expression. Colours, sizes and shapes of figures, positions of limbs and facial expressions, and attributes of gods and demons, are all strictly codified. The painter's individual talent is expressed entirely in his skill in giving life to these traditional forms. 'Creative genius' and 'originality' in the Western sense (concepts which became important in European art only after the Renaissance) are not an issue here. The result is that frescoes painted by monks in this century are practically indistinguishable from those painted five hundred years ago. If it were not for the brighter, fresher colours you would not be able to tell them apart.

Tankas are sacred paintings in gouache on paper or cotton. They are attached to long silk brocade hangings with a stick at each end to form banners for the decoration of temples, prayer rooms or shrines in private houses. Until quite recently *tankas* were only painted by monks, but now lay schools of painting have opened up, a sign of change in an apparently unchanging land.

Chandigarh was built in the 1950s by the Swiss architect Le Corbusier to a plan based on the human body. One part of the city represents the heart, another the brain, and so on. Intended to be the capital of Punjab, Chandigarh is now the joint capital of both Punjab and Haryana. The city is a celebrated example of modernism in architecture, designed with little regard for local traditions of building.

The Tribal Lands of North-East India

North-East India is one of the most politically, culturally and geographically complex regions of the world. Its landscapes range from the majesty of Mount Kanchenjunga, the world's third highest peak, to the steamy flooded plains of the Ganges delta and the jungles of Orissa. Ethnically and linguistically it is a hotch-potch too, with primitive tribes such as the Bondos living alongside the highly civilised Bengalis, whose literature and film industry allow them, with some justification, to regard themselves as India's cultural élite. Politically, the region includes two independent nations (Bhutan and Bangladesh) and ten states of the Indian Union: West Bengal, Manipur, Tripura, Assam, Meghalaya, Nagaland, Sikkim, Orissa, Arunachal Pradesh and Mizoram. Governments range from monarchy in Bhutan to the Communist administration in West Bengal.

Bhutan is an underpopulated, largely mountainous kingdom of some 1.4 million people between Assam and Tibet. Its early history is unknown, but its present political system arose from wars between provincial governors which plagued the country for several centuries until a hereditary and absolute monarchy was established in 1907.

Bangladesh has existed as an independent state since 1971. Between 1947 and 1971 it was in the anomalous position of being a part of Pakistan, even though it was a thousand miles from the main part of the country and had a different language and culture. Independence was gained through a war with Pakistan, won with the help of India. It is densely populated, with 110 million inhabitants living in an area not much bigger than that of England.

The neighbouring state of West Bengal, with the great metropolis and port of Calcutta, is the economic powerhouse of the region, although its partition from East Bengal in 1912 by the British, and the subsequent movement of frontiers and peoples, have had a deeply unsettling effect. Orissa, to the south, is largely agricultural although its industrial base is developing

Bengalis account for almost the whole population of independent Bangladesh and the Indian state of West Bengal: a total of more than 160 million, making them one of the most numerous peoples in the world. Of Indo-Aryan language and race, they are particularly proud of their culture, which includes world-famous figures such as the writer Tagore and the film director Satyajit Ray.

Calcutta is a monstrous megalopolis teeming with life. Fantastic wealth exists side by side with the deepest poverty. In this city of more than 10 million inhabitants, moving about is difficult. Cars, buses, trams and rickshaws thread their way through the crowd in a nightmarish mêlée.

You can see cycle rickshaws and motor rickshaws in all Indian towns, but the genuine rickshaw familiar in China and South-East Asia can be found only in Calcutta, providing a meagre income for tens of thousands of families.

fast as a result of its wealth in minerals. Assam, to the north, prospers from exports of tea and oil. The smallest of India's states, Sikkim, lies to the west of Bhutan and occupies only 2739 square miles. This Himalayan kingdom was ruled by a feudal monarch from the mid-17th century until 1975 when its people voted for union with India. The population is 75 per cent Nepali, and their vote proved decisive in the 1975 constitutional change, overriding the wishes of the Tibetans and Lepchas who supported the hereditary ruler.

Meghalaya is another recent creation, seceding from the state of Assam in 1972. Sometimes called 'the Scotland of India' for the mountainous beauty of its landscape, Meghalaya is peopled by some of the most ancient tribes in India. They were given special protection by Nehru, but feeling threatened by the imposition of Assamese as the official language in 1960, they demanded – and finally achieved – autonomy. Of the remaining states, Mizoram and Arunachal Pradesh were also part of Assam until 1972. The most unsettled of the states is Nagaland, which has fifteen major tribes in an area scarcely bigger than Northern Ireland. Their representatives were persuaded to join the Indian Union as a separate state in 1963, but dissidents within Nagaland continued a violent campaign for full independence. This campaign, discredited when it was proved to be backed by the Chinese, has now almost died down, although a core of militancy remains.

Darjiling and Sikkim

As you step from the aeroplane at Bagdogra, the first thing you see are the words 'altitude 214 feet'. There is something odd about this, for Bagdogra is the airport for Bhutan, Sikkim and eastern Nepal – all mountain areas.

Bagdogra, however, sits in a flat, monotonous landscape with a climate that is hot in spring, oppressive in summer, and just about bearable in winter. Three and a half hours' drive away is Darjiling, more than 7000 feet above sea level, with its tea plantations and the Kanchenjunga massif dominating the horizon. The Himalayas rear up from the plain here, with little in the way of foothills. Darjiling was developed by the British when they planted tea here in the 1840s. Much of its architecture is still redolent of British rule, including the names of its principal sights: the Mall, Observatory Hill, the Shrubbery, the Planters' Club and the Lloyd Botanical Gardens.

Beyond Darjiling the road descends, then crosses a lush and fertile valley before climbing again towards Sikkim. Around Gangtok, the capital of Sikkim, the landscape is reminiscent of Darjiling – gently rolling hills with terraced tea plantations. If you want to go farther into the mountains the best way is to walk: a five-day trek up to Dzongri, 16,400 feet above sea level and set in an awe-inspiring amphitheatre of peaks.

There is no way through from Sikkim to Bhutan. Instead, you have to go back to 'altitude 214 feet', then east along the foothills to the frontier post at Phuntsholing. From here you can climb through

Almost everywhere in the back streets of Calcutta you find these small temples. At the bottom is Siva, who can be recognised by the three horizontal bands on his brow. Above him, a shell and a wheel on either side of a winged figure (Garuda) identify Vishnu, who is seated between two goddesses. The street stall sells tea and yoghurt.

Calcutta's buses are designed to transport the maximum number of people over short distances. Anyone who can hangs on to the sides.

forested mountains to the high valleys of Thimbu, Paro, Tongsa and Bumtang, with a sensation of penetrating a primeval, untouched world.

After the pass at Chapcha (8200 feet), the road enters the valley of Paro, then Thimbu: dazzling clearings of green fields and rice paddies among forests of conifers, rhododendrons and giant magnolias. Another pass separates Thimbu from Punakha – a former capital – which is a kind of Himalayan tropical garden, where the

rhododendrons unexpectedly give way to Barbary figs.

Returning to the plain and moving eastwards again, you come to Assam. Although this is another famous tea-growing area, the land is flat and uninspiring. A few clumps of sal trees break the monotony. The city of Gauhati, on the river Brahmaputra is worth a visit, as are the wildlife parks of Kaziranga and Manas, where tigers, golden langur monkeys, pygmy hogs and the fabled *Rhinoceros Unicornis*, India's one-horned

Peasant farmers in Bangladesh, where agriculture is mostly practised in forest clearings.

rhinoceros, may be viewed from observation lodges or the back of an elephant. The game reserves also have a serious purpose; without them it is likely that the Asian rhinoceros, which Marco Polo believed to be the legendary unicorn, would have become extinct.

Farther south, the two Bengals, Bangladesh and West Bengal, have a landscape where earth and water meet and mix to create rich plains irrigated by the Ganges and Brahmaputra and regularly flooded after the monsoon rains. Near here (though just over the border in Meghalaya) is the rainiest spot on earth: Cherrapunji. Here, on the southern slope of the Shilling plateau, the rising monsoon wind is cooled quickly, releasing vast quantities of water from the clouds. The scene is vividly described by Alexander Frater in his book, *Chasing the Monsoon* (1990): 'A fountain of dense black cloud came spiralling over the hills, then rose steeply into the sky. It formed a kind of tent, apex high overhead, sides unrolling right to the ground. It was very dark inside but I could just discern, trooping towards us, an armada of shadowy, galleon-like vessels with undersides festooned with writhing cables of water. They gave off thundery rumbles and a noise like discharging hydrants, the rain descending in hissing vertical rafts of solid matter that lathered the earth and made the spokes of the umbrella, under which I had taken shelter, bend like saplings.'

While Manchester, one of the wettest cities in Britain, has an average annual rainfall of 34 inches, Cherrapunji has 450 inches a year.

Over the Bengal plains lies Calcutta, a sprawling metropolis of some 12 million inhabitants whose unhealthy climate, crowds, slums, dirt and beggars have made it a symbol of Third World misery. Yet it continues to attract country people looking for jobs, as well as visitors who find its culture and way of life uniquely vital. The city was founded in 1690 as a trading post by an official of the English East India company, Job Charnock. He chose the position, 80 miles upstream from the mouth of the Hugli (Hooghly) river, partly for defensive and partly for commercial reasons: soon the entire trade of Bengal with the outside world was to pass through the city. In 1775 Robert Clive described Calcutta as 'one of the most wicked places in the universe'. From 1772 to 1912 it was the capital of British India, with flourishing commerce, banking and insurance, and a wealth of palatial architecture. At about the same time as the British moved the capital to Delhi in 1912, Calcutta's leading commercial position began to be eroded and social problems – overcrowding, riots and conflicts between

Very few Indians fish, because they prefer trade or agriculture. A few villages along the coasts of the Sea of Oman and the Bay of Bengal survive with difficulty from the sale of their catches. Fishermen have to face the dangerous rollers of the Bay of Bengal in small boats like this.

Muslims and Hindus – increased. The partition of Bengal in 1947 reduced the city's importance further, and economic stagnation in the 1960s, as well as refugees from the Bangladesh war of 1971, added to its problems. However, the Communist government of West Bengal improved matters through public works and social reconstruction in the 1980s. Despite its grim reputation, few who know the city would disagree with Rudyard Kipling's verdict: 'There is only one city in India. Bombay is too green, too pretty, and too strugglesome; and Madras died ever so long ago. Let us take our hats off to Calcutta, the many-sided, the smoky, the magnificent . . .'

South of this hive of struggling humanity is Orissa, by comparison a haven of peace. Bhubaneshwar, the

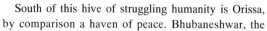

Many of India's tea pickers are recruited in Nepal where labour is cheap.

Tea, a bush from the camellia family, has small white flowers which are not used. The tea pickers pluck off the newest bud on a branch and the two small leaves which come with it. The harvest goes on continuously from spring to autumn. In winter, the bushes are clipped regularly, with pruning taking place every six or seven years.

The tea harvest in Bangladesh (above) and in the region of Darjiling (left). The quality of the tea varies according to the altitude at which it grows. Tea from Bangladesh, Assam and West Bengal (which are at low altitudes) is of poorer quality, but plentiful and cheap. It is black and tastes bitter because of the high tannin content. Darjiling tea, on the other hand, is a high-altitude tea. Its low tannin content gives it a light colour and a strong aroma. Most teas drunk in the West are a mixture of teas from high and low altitudes.

The Bhutanese show their ingenuity and originality best in their architecture. The large wooden structures are made without nails and the roof is kept in place by stones. Generally, the ground floor is occupied by animals, the first floor by people, and the loft is used for drying straw and meat.

capital, is surrounded by orchards and mango trees. There were once over a thousand temples here, and there are still plenty left.

Judged by its statistics, Orissa is the poorest state in India. Yet a visitor gains the impression of a fertile, calm and hospitable land. Here is the site of a great religious festival, the Rath Yatra, celebrated at the Jagannath temple every summer for the past thousand years. The chariots of the gods – and particularly of the deity Jagannath himself – more than 40 feet high, have given us the word juggernaut for something far less colourful and pleasant.

Fortresses and straw huts

The variety of climate, landscape and cultures in North-East India is reflected in the houses, which are based on the materials available. In Bangladesh, Orissa and West Bengal, floors and walls are made of earth, given a coat of cattle dung, then painted with whitewash or brown ochre, often with geometric patterns to liven them up. Painted doors add to the picturesque effect. The roof is thatched with straw.

In Bangladesh, where the land is prone to flooding, and in Arunachal Pradesh where wild animals are still a

threat to human habitation, houses are often set on stilts. The Adis in Arunachal Pradesh build their homes on platforms supported by massive teak pillars. Around the house is a balcony with a bamboo rail – bamboo being cheaper than teak. Branches and trunks are lashed together with oso, a pliant form of cane which is tough and water-resistant. The roof is covered with leaves.

The Nagas are thought to be the ancestors of numerous Indonesian peoples including the architecturally inventive Torajas. Naga houses are more complex than the average dwelling in these parts. Between the structural timbers they stretch bamboo

trellises made of five interwoven strips. Nets hung above ground outside are used for drying edibles in the sun. A large cylindrical drum close to the front door is beaten to signal good news or to call the family together in case of an emergency.

The Lepchas of Sikkim live in rectangular houses that point north-south. The ground floor, which is for animals, is built of stone, with one side open to the east – an auspicious direction. The upper levels – two rooms with an attic above – are made of wood and bamboo with plaited leaves for the roof. A local architect oversees the work on the ground floor: four large tree trunks stuck firmly in the earth, and the stone walls built between them. When this section of the house is complete, the architect leaves the rest up to the family to finish.

Access to the upper floor is by a stairway or notched tree trunk set against the east side of the house. The first room you enter is the kitchen, where every member of the family has his or her allotted place for both eating and sleeping. A wooden partition separates this from the second room, which is a prayer room. The Lepchas are Buddhists in the Tibetan tradition, and only *lamas* are allowed to sleep in here.

In the Nicobar Islands, 700 miles out into the Bay of Bengal, the aboriginals live in conical straw huts on stilts. They go in and out through a trap door in the floor reached by a ladder. The *Ongas*, in the Andaman Islands nearby, simply fashion two sloping roofs of branches and leaves in the shape of a ridge tent or inverted V, with both ends left open.

Houses in Bhutan are generally isolated since the

The Bhutanese harvest twice a year. There is a crop of rice at the end of the monsoon, and a crop of wheat in spring. Their agricultural methods are archaic. Here, a peasant woman uses a winnowing basket to separate the grain from the chaff. She is wearing a jacket (tego) *over her traditional dress* (kira).

Bhutanese consider life in villages undesirable. The pride of their architecture are the *dzongs*: fortress monasteries similar to the castles of medieval Europe. Once semi-independent, the *dzongs* are now provincial capitals. The structure consists of a square or rectangular complex of several storeys with internal courtyards. Inside the monumental gateway are the secular parts of the *dzong*: the provincial administration, the governor and the law courts. After that comes the monastic section, where the monks share a residential block with many of the country's lay population. This curious arrangement reflects the social structure of the kingdom, which is a mixture of feudal and monastic.

Undoubtedly the most extraordinary feature of the *dzongs* is not their colossal dimensions, their frescoes or carved woodwork, but the fact that they are built without the use of a single nail. The structural timbers interlock and are secured with pegs, and the roof tiles are held in place by stones.

An Asian Babel

Apart from the 160 million Bengalis in the plains – who make up the vast majority of the populations of West Bengal and Bangladesh, as well as minorities in Assam, Tripura and other states – a bewildering range of peoples and tribes live in the hills and mountains of this part of India. A glance at an ethnic map of India shows the thickest cluster of names in this region: the Bondo Kond, Saora, Juang and Ho in Orissa; the Kharia,

Munda, Bhumij, Oraon, Santal and Maler in Bihar; the Garo, the Khasi, the Bodo in Meghalaya; and so on to the borders of Burma, China and Tibet.

The Khasis of Meghalaya are thought to have originated farther east, since their language belongs to the Mon-Khmer group, as do the languages of Burma, Vietnam and Cambodia. The Khasis are unusual in having a matrilineal system of inheritance: property, names and tribal office are passed on from mother to daughter, not father to son. (Curiously, both property and office are in practice administered or held by men appointed by the women.) Young men and women are free to choose their partners in marriage. Eldest daughters are particularly sought after, since they generally inherit their family's property. Divorce and remarriage are also allowed.

Despite the 'modern' appearance of these customs, Khasi traditions recall more ancient ways. Soothsayers play an important part in everyday life and child sacrifice to the serpent god U-thlen is said to take place even today. Whether this is true or an invention of over-zealous Christian missionaries – who have had considerable success in converting the Khasis and disrupting their way of life – it is impossible to say.

Political decisions are made by a council of elders under the presidency of the oldest member of the community. The council's decisions are then promulgated in the name of U-Blei-Nang-Pha, or God the creator.

A Khasi father will choose the name of his child by reciting a list of names while pouring a glass of alcohol.

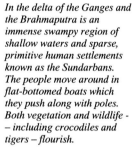

In the delta of the Ganges and the Brahmaputra is an immense swampy region of shallow waters and sparse, primitive human settlements known as the Sundarbans. The people move around in flat-bottomed boats which they push along with poles. Both vegetation and wildlife - – including crocodiles and tigers – flourish.

The name that he is saying as the last drop falls is the one given to the child.

The Garo people, also from Meghalaya, believe that life is guided by spirits, both good and evil. Each is associated with a different aspect of existence. The god of creation for example, Tantara Rabunga, protects the Garas from sickness and death. Dances and songs are

and head-shrinkers. They have now given up this practice, although they retain others. When a young man in the Angami Naga tribe wants to marry a girl, he goes to her father and asks his permission. The girl's father then slits the throat of a chicken, and if the animal crosses its legs in a certain way in its death agony, the marriage is approved.

performed in praise of this benevolent god and in the hope of a rich harvest.

Like the Khasis, the Garos allow free choice of marriage partners – free at least on the girl's side. If a girl wants to marry a young man she has him kidnapped by her friends and keeps him prisoner until he accepts. Unlike the Khasis, where the man goes to live in a house owned by the wife, the Garo women go to live with their husbands. Even so, every husband has to spend the first month of his married life living with his in-laws so as to get to know them properly.

The Nagas, who live in the extreme north-east of India, once had a ferocious reputation as head-hunters

A more rational 'test' for a prospective couple is organised by the Nongsen Nagas, who send the pair on a commercial expedition. If this is successful, they can marry. Sex before marriage is actively discouraged, and girls are shaven-headed until puberty to reduce their attractiveness to boys.

Divorce is easy, and a woman may even claim back her dowry. The value of a dowry depends on the girl's level of education and practical accomplishments, such as her ability to weave. A man's value was once assessed by more brutal means: the number of heads he had cut off in fights with other tribes and retained as trophies. A man with only one or two heads would find

This woman and her children belong to one of the tribes which live in the hills near the town of Chittagong, in the east of Bangladesh.

it extremely hard to tempt a woman into marriage.

The Nagas eat practically anything that moves – even dogs and crows. Convention dictates that delicacies such as skin and tripe are reserved for the chief or guests. There are also certain taboos: pregnant women avoid eating monkeys in case their child turns into an idiot, and neither tiger nor leopard is eaten for fear of it turning the consumer wild.

Assamese women have none of the power enjoyed by their neighbours in the Khasi and Garo tribes. If a woman commits an offence, she will pay half the fine a man would pay. This may sound like a benefit, but it diminishes the status of women by implying that they have only half the responsibility of men.

The Assamese will never cut bamboo on a Tuesday or Saturday, believing that the spirits who live in the thickets will do them harm on those days. Tuesdays and Saturdays are also regarded as inauspicious for starting a project or piece of work. A cloth thrown over a snake and then worn about the body brings good luck in love and victory in war. Owl meat is eaten as an aphrodisiac, but if an owl flies into your house you are in for a spell of misfortune.

These customs and beliefs are more or less common to all the tribes of Assam, although every tribe has its own individual traditions. Among the Hindu tribes, young brides and their mothers always fast the night before a wedding. During the ceremony they throw rice at each other's faces to ward off evil spirits. In the Bodo tribe a hopeful young bachelor will go to the home of the girl he loves and leave a pair of silver bracelets and a bottle of wine on the roof. If these presents are not returned within a week, his offer of marriage is considered accepted.

When a widowed man and woman want to marry, the widow cooks a dish of chicken and rice and the widower approaches her house on hands and knees. He starts miaowing like a cat, begging to be allowed in. The widow bars the door. The man walks once round the house then tries again. Again the widow refuses. The man sets off round the house again, miaows a third time and is again refused. This process is repeated until the seventh time, when the widow relents and serves him the rice and chicken. From this moment they are considered married.

Among the Rabha tribe, divorce has a ceremony of its own. The husband and wife stand face to face, each clutching a betel leaf. They then snatch at each other's leaves. The one who gets the largest piece is allowed to remarry, while the other has to remain single.

A peasant house made of earth, thatch and bamboo, with a curious earthen fireplace (right, foreground). Behind the fireplace is a round-bottomed pan used for frying. Near the door is a copper container for drinking water. The women decorate the walls with whitewash to attract the good graces of the gods.

Fifty tribes in Arunachal Pradesh have different languages or dialects as well as tribal customs. The Mogpas are lamaistic Buddhists known for their hospitality. A stranger passing through their villages is greeted with music in carpeted ceremonial tents. They live in beautifully decorated wooden houses with wall-paintings depicting scenes from the life of Buddha.

The Daflas and Miris, who live in the hills, wear their hair tied in a topknot over their foreheads, behind which sits a pointed hat bristling with porcupine quills and the claws of birds of prey. The women sheathe their bodies in dresses made from rings of flexible bamboo or reeds.

Boys of the Adi tribe go around naked and sleep in a dormitory until they reach puberty. At puberty they leave the dormitory and begin to wear clothes, which entails paying a 'clothing tax' to the chief. Other tribes, such as the Wanchoos, never wear any clothes at all, but only ornaments made of feathers, horn, ivory or bone.

The Mishmis live in scattered houses which scarcely form communities of any kind. Adults and children alike smoke tobacco and opium out of little silver pipes which they keep by them constantly.

The Idu Mishmis forbid their women to eat meat, believing that it makes them sterile. There is also a taboo on eating the meat of tigers and *langurs* since these are totems – animals with which the members of the tribe believe themselves to be connected in a mystical kinship.

Despite this diversity of customs and beliefs, the tribes of Arunachal Pradesh all permit sexual relations before marriage.

Festival of the full moon

Farther south, in Orissa, several tribes still live in the jungle. These include the Gadabas, the Koyas and Bondos. The Bondos have retained most of their traditional ways. They grow maize and rice, and raise cattle and goats for trade. They cut down an area of forest, burn the wood and grow crops in the ash for two or three years, then move on. There are around 5000 Bondos, living in 15 villages in the region of Khairaput in the extreme south of Orissa. A hereditary monarch rules over them, ensuring respect for the traditions of the tribe. Each village has an elected chief – usually the strongest or most dominating personality, a man with the means to impose his will on others. His office lasts as long as his strength. As soon as this goes, he is voted out.

A great religious festival takes place at the full moon in June–July. This is an excuse for drunkenness on a grand scale, using a flower-based alcoholic beverage called *mahuwa* which is also found in Rajasthan. The drinking often leads to fights, since the Bondos flare up at the slightest provocation when in their cups. Disagreement about the division of produce between landowners and share-croppers, for instance, can degenerate into a bloodbath. This festival of the full

The awning of straw, held up by bamboo poles placed in front of the house, gives shade during the day and a cool place to sleep at night. The woman is winnowing; the large baskets are used to store the grain when it has been separated from the chaff.

The people of Orissa add to their normal food by catching a few small fish with these simple nets with circular wooden frames.

moon is the only time when the Bondos eat meat. It lasts from seven to fifteen days, depending on the stocks of food available. When the food and drink runs out, the celebrations stop.

Polygamy is tolerated by the Bondos but rarely practised, on the grounds of expense. January is the month for getting married, the ceremony taking between two and five days. Women tend to be older than their husbands; often the wife is 20, say, and the husband only 12. Divorce is frequent, perhaps because of such mismatches between sexually mature girls and pre-adolescent boys. When there is a divorce, the father takes care of any children aged three and over, while the mother retains any infants. The Bondos practise a mixture of Hinduism and paganism based on the natural elements. They pray to the sun, the mountains and rivers. Their priests are also their doctors. When a person dies, his body is burned and coins are thrown into the fire – though they are recovered afterwards when the ashes are cold.

They walk about in a state of near-nudity, occasionally wearing a small loincloth. The women wear long glassware necklaces and enormous rings around their necks. They are more or less self-sufficient in food and buy little at markets apart from coconuts,

dried fish, brightly coloured cloth, glass beads for necklaces, cigarettes and umbrellas. They also make their own giant cigars.

A timeless people

South of Burma more than 250 islands run parallel to the Malay peninsula. These are the Nicobar and Andaman Islands, which belong to India. There are still a few tribes left here, but their numbers are dwindling. There were 3500 inhabitants in 1859, but only 24 at the census of 1971. Most of the Andamanese are Negritos, similar in build to the pygmies of the Philippines or

A market in the region of Shillong, the capital of Meghalaya (a state recently created to safeguard the independence of the tribes which live in it). The Garo and Khasi peoples who live in the state are very skilled at weaving cane, reed and rattan – some examples of which can be seen here.

This woman belongs to one of the many tribes which live in Assam. Of the two rich necklaces she is wearing, one is silver and the other coral. Coral is brought from the Bay of Bengal and was sometimes taken by caravan as far as Tibet and China.

A working elephant in Assam. Sadly such sights are becoming rarer every day in India.

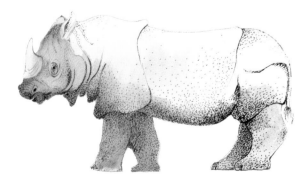

Only a few hundred examples of the Asian rhinoceros exist in the reserves of Nepalese Terai (Citwan), Bengal (Jaldapara), and Assam (Kaziranga, Manas). This rhinoceros is different from its African cousin in that it has only one horn. The horn is the main reason why the rhinoceros has been hunted almost to extinction. In some places it is mistakenly thought that a powder of ground rhino horn has aphrodisiac powers. Poachers can sell each horn for tens of thousands of rupees.

Africa and rarely growing taller than five feet. Tribes such as the Onges have survived by attacking visitors with showers of arrows. They go naked except for a small loincloth and a few jewels. They smear their faces with clay or a mixture of plant extracts and turtle fat, changing the patterns and colours of their face paint according to the occasion – hunting, feasting, mourning, and so on. In the absence of clothes, face-painting provides a means of expressing their tastes, feelings and reactions to circumstances.

The Onges live by hunting and gathering, fishing and catching shellfish. They use bamboo arrows with tips made of hardwood, shell or iron salvaged from wrecks. Different arrowheads will be used to hunt wild boar, fish and turtles, and they have harpoons up to 16 feet long for killing *dugongs* – large marine mammals similar in appearance to seals. They have little sense of time, and a boar hunt can go on happily for several days. They have no jobs or occupations apart from catching and collecting food. Their cooking is simple: having killed their prey, they roast it whole – skin, fur, guts, giblets and all.

Yet perhaps the most extraordinary thing about these people is the way that they have no hierarchy, and no leaders or chiefs. Nor do they have private property: they simply take a canoe when they need one.

They treat their great god Paluga as a friend, thanking him when things go well, complaining when they go badly. There are no offerings, supplications or sacrifices, just conversations. They are truly relics of a lost world.

A king in robe and socks

The Bhutanese are among the most 'feudal' of all the peoples of Eastern India. There was a state here as long ago as the 10th century, but apart from conflicts in defence of its territory, its contacts with the outside world have been few and cautious. Bhutan has in many ways stayed locked in the Middle Ages – a real-life version of the fictional Shangri-La. The whole of society looks up to one figure: the king. Everyone else has a precise place in the hierarchy, marked by coloured stripes woven into a scarf that each citizen possesses and has to wear every time he or she enters a *dzong* or monastic stronghold. On visits to the king, this index of social rank is reinforced and elaborated with different lengths of cuffs and collars.

Apart from these minor variations, most men wear the same clothes, including the king: robes with belts (*kho*) rather like dressing gowns, and knee-length socks. The only difference is in the quality of the cloth: certain valleys, such as Bumtang, are known for their fine textiles. Although women, too, have robes, fastened at the shoulder with clasps, theirs are ornamented with trimmings of various kinds – embroideries or brocades. They also wear heavy necklaces of gold, coral and turquoise.

Every year, in autumn, a feast called Tsechu takes place at the dzong (castle) of Thimbu, the capital of Bhutan. On this occasion the monks dress in silk brocades and masks, and mime mythological scenes.

Two typical instruments of lamaist music. In the foreground are two oboes, and, partially hidden in the background, a long trumpet. The musician in the foreground wears a scarf on his shoulder which indicates his rank. It is obligatory for all male Bhutanis to wear them inside the dzong.

Monks in the monastery of Pumtek mix tsampa flour to make the cone-shaped cakes that are used in a religious ceremony. Recently constructed, it is a copy of a great Tibetan monastery belonging to the famous Karnapa sect.

The hookah is the Indian version of a smoking apparatus found throughout the Muslim-Arab world from Morocco to Pakistan. The spread of the hookah into India followed the same routes as Islam.

The national sport is archery, practised according to the riskiest rules imaginable. Instead of stationary targets, they have two teams who stand facing each other and take turns to shoot. Each bowman aims for one of the opponents, who has to try to dodge the oncoming arrow without moving his feet.

The Buddhist monks are as carefully ranked as the rest of society. In a nation of about 1.4 million people, there are 1300 *dzongs*, which dominate the countryside as castles once did in Europe. Most of the people are Buddhist – although more primitive pagan beliefs influence their religion. The brightest sons of families are sent, sometimes when they are only three years old,

to live in the *dzongs* and become monks. Monks ruled the country until 1907, when they were replaced by an absolute monarch, the Dragon King. The present ruler, the youthful Jigme Singye Wangchuk, follows the regal customs established by his great-grandfather, dispensing justice and even marital advice to all supplicants.

At the head of the monks is the Jey Khenpo, who officiates at the coronation of a new king (the present king was crowned in 1974). His headquarters is at Punakha, the religious capital. Religious festivals are organised regularly in each *dzong*, the monks wearing brocades and masks representing mythological figures such as Padma Sambhava, who is said to have

In Bengal the shankaris *are a special caste. Their name comes from* shanka, *which means 'shell', because they make bracelets from sea shells. They cut the shells with enormous crescent-shaped blades, then polish them. For the richest clients they decorate them with gold wire or gold leaf, while the poorest make do with a coat of lacquer. The* shankari *sometimes adds a sculpted head of a* makara, *a mythical animal which resembles an alligator. When they are married, the Hindu women of Bengal wear a pair of bracelets made of sea shells, given to them by their father at the moment of their engagement.*

introduced Buddhism to the Himalayas in the 8th century, and Padma Karpo, founder of the so-called 'Southern' Drukpa sect.

The name 'Drukpa' means 'People of the Dragon', from a dragon which appeared to Padma Karpo's spiritual predecessor. There are several Drukpa sects, from the non-reformed Nyingmapas who believe in magic and sorcery to the reformed who claim to have gone back to the original teachings of the Buddha. The name of Bhutan in the local language is Druk-Yul or 'Country of the Dragon'.

Each *dzong* celebrates between one and three festivals a year. Most are to commemorate the birth of Padma Sambhava, portrayed on a huge embroidered banner more than 30 feet square which is hung from the walls of the *dzong* throughout the festival.

By the standard measures of our so-called advanced civilisations, the people of Bhutan are among the poorest on earth. But there is no starvation in their remote Himalayan country; there is no unemployment, no begging and virtually no crime. They are wary of wealth, because of the damage it would cause to their cultural traditions.

The decorative arts

Examples of pottery in the three large states of Bangladesh, Orissa and West Bengal have survived from at least 2000 years ago. They range from cooking pots with covers, large storage jars for grain, narrow-necked pitchers for carrying and conserving water, bowls for yoghurt and troughs for feeding and watering cattle, to ritual objects such as oil lamps and clay images of gods.

While the potter works at his wheel, his wife and children make little clay toys, horses, elephants, people and birds. The human figures usually represent a mother holding a child in her arms. These are used as dolls by the children.

Birds are quick and easy to make: a drop-shaped

Because few tourists go to Assam, foreigners know little about its silks. The primitive loom seen here is made of bamboo; it has several rails, which allow highly elaborate work.

Bangladeshi women wear the sari. The woman on the left is spinning with a simple apparatus consisting of a bamboo spindle shaped like a closed umbrella. On the right, a large reel takes up the thread to make the hanks.

lump of clay for the body, three smaller lumps for the wings and head, two tiny balls for the eyes and a pair of twigs for the feet. Figures like this have a long ancestry, and were once used by Hindus as ritual objects to attract the favour of the gods. Models of other animals such as elephants were – and still are – used simply as toys.

The people of Orissa, the Oriyas, have developed a number of crafts of their own. In the village of Pipli, for example, near the coast between Puri, Konarak and Bhubaneshwar, they make umbrellas, parasols, lampshades and wall hangings from patchwork. It is not odd pieces of cloth sewn together to form a random pattern, but carefully composed scenes featuring human and animal figures in vibrant reds, yellows and blues.

You find the same bright colours in the Oriyas' paintings, which are done in thick gouache on waxed cloth. The subjects are almost always mythological or divine: Rama with his wife and brother, or Krishna in his local manifestation as Jagannath. Jagannath is a highly popular figure for depiction in other media too, such as clay and wood sculpture.

Jewellery, jute and joy for life

A less colourful but no less striking art form – engraving on palm leaves – is practised in a number of remote Oriyan villages. Again, mythological themes dominate. The images are cut with extraordinary delicacy into the leaves using a stylet or fine graving tool, then dusted with black powder. This powder is wiped off the surface of the leaf, leaving the engraved lines, where the powder remains, showing black. Several palm leaves are then strung together to make large composite panels like blinds. A similar technique was once used in Sri Lanka for producing books.

Bengali jewellers and metalworkers can create practically anything in their workshops – necklaces, bangles, cooking pots, bells, nutcrackers, lamps, trays, vases, hookahs, rice scoops, spoons, shovels and knives. Dhaka (Dacca), the capital of Bangladesh, is renowned for filigree jewellery, with more than 60 specialist shops. The craftsman at work is an intriguing sight, with his blow-lamp and coils of silver and gold wire which he threads over bracelets, necklaces and rings in patterns of swirls. The intricacies of the jeweller's designs are reminiscent of the all-white muslin embroideries known as *shikankaris* which are the pride of Dhaka homes.

Many married Hindu women in Bengal wear conch-shell bracelets, given by a father to his daughter when she is about to be married. She wears them for the rest of her life – or until her husband dies. The conch shells are polished and cut by a special caste, the *shankaris* (from *shanka* meaning 'conch'). The bracelets may be covered with lacquer or decorated with threads of gold. Sometimes the *shankari* will add a carved head of a *makara* – a mythical beast similar to a crocodile.

Jute – a tough natural fibre normally used for making sacks and rope, and one of Calcutta's principal exports – is also used in West Bengal and Bangladesh to create macramé (known locally as *sikha*), a type of knotted string mesh where the knots form decorative patterns: flowers, leaves, palm trees, pomegranates and so on. *Sikha* nets are hung from the ceilings of Bengali houses to store food out of reach of crawling insects. They are also exported to the West for hanging flower baskets and indoor plants.

You could not have a better symbol of India: a land where even the most unlikely material – from cow dung to porcupine quills – is used with amazing inventiveness to keep life going or to make it more beautiful.

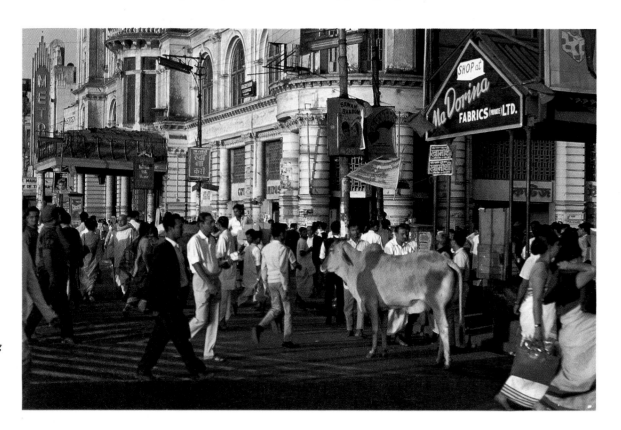

People walking in the evening sun in Chowringhee, one of the main streets of Calcutta. The presence of cows in the streets of the city has always surprised foreigners.

Nepal

Nepal is a long finger of land, just 100 miles wide, flanked by
Chinese Tibet and India, but its landscape ranges from the pinnacles
of the eastern Himalayas – including Mount Everest – to the Terai,
or southern flatlands, where the lush jungle is home to tigers,
elephants and rare Indian rhinoceroses. It is an under-developed
country, with few natural resources and a population subsisting on
agricultural smallholdings. Famous as much for its native flowers –
the rhododendron and azalea – as for its intrepid Gurkha warriors,
Nepal is a tiny oasis of unspoilt beauty that is only now starting to
develop an independence from its mighty neighbours.

A Sherpa herdsman milks a nak, or female yak. In these high mountain regions, crops are few and not always reliable, so people depend on their livestock for food and drink. The milk of the nak – and of the various yak cross-breeds – is made into clarified butter, or ghee, and cheese.

Previous page:
Caravans of pack animals still make their way along the ancient trade routes through the Himalayas, though nowadays their loads include modern fertilisers and paraffin as well as traditional goods such as salt. The ponies and mules leading the processions wear eye-catching red-dyed yaks' tails. The porters accompanying them on foot use the namlo *headband to help them to carry their load.*

The Land of Eternal Snows

The rice-growing plains of the Terai region, spreading out for 500 miles along Nepal's southern frontier with India, are the mountain kingdom at its most domesticated, and yet most diverse. In season, the strangely luminous flowers of the kapok-bearing *simal* tree stud the landscape with flashes of brilliant red, rivalled only by the blossoms of the *palash* ('flame of the forest') tree. Above, squabbling, many-hued flocks of parakeets scatter from copses of mango trees, while in marshy areas beds of reeds give off silvery reflections. In this glorious setting, bounded to the north by the rising flanks of Nepal's central hills, people live life at the pace of the ox-drawn cart or the leisurely flow of rivers meandering on their way to join the Ganges. It is a region of villages with small, mud-built, thatched houses, dotted here and there with stands of the distinctive sal tree – tall, straight and with a wood that is much used as a building material.

Stretching out in the Terai's centre is the Chitwan National Park, once a royal hunting ground, now a popular tourist destination. Thousands of visitors flock through the park each year, but have not yet managed to destroy its magic. Here, the specially reared royal elephants roam free, except when needed for a coronation or other great occasion. For these events, the beasts are decked out with gold and brocade, and form the centrepieces of magnificent processions. During the rest of the year, their only adornment is the dust clinging to their gnarled skins, suitably gilded in the evenings by the rays of the setting sun.

The park is also one of the last refuges of the Asian one-horned rhinoceros, whose skin is so tough that Nepali warriors of old made shields from it to protect themselves from sabre-wielding Mogul invaders from India. More recently, the species has come under threat of extinction, thanks to a Chinese belief that its horn has aphrodisiac qualities when ground to a fine powder. The park is also home to leopards, tigers, many kinds of deer (including the *chital* or spotted deer, the stumpy hog deer and the well-named barking deer), boars, bears and monkeys. Birds include wild peacocks, cranes, egrets, kingfishers, jungle cocks and wild duck. River banks shelter crocodiles, including the narrow-jawed, fish-eating *gharial*, which can reach 20 feet long and is not averse to adding human flesh to its diet.

Jungle still covers much of the park – as it once did most of the Terai. The thin undergrowth is scented with sprays of jasmine. In open spaces, tufts of elephant grass can grow up to 33 feet high. The greatest danger to humans in the Terai used to be the malarial mosquito. Only after this was eradicated earlier this century did the local population begin to swell, to the extent that a third of all Nepali people now live in the Terai. As a result, in most areas rice paddies have taken over from the jungle – for centuries the country's first line of defence against invaders.

The so-called hills – *pahar* in Nepali – that form the country's backbone are mountains of modest size (by Himalayan standards, at least) that spread out on either side of the central Kathmandu Valley. Most are inhabited up to around 8000 feet above sea level, and above that their slopes and peaks provide summer grazing up to about 15,000 feet. The locals believe the more impressive bluffs and outcrops in these higher altitudes are dwelling places of the gods. Every year, at times determined by the cycles of the moon, villagers gather at the holy places for *jaatras* or festivals. According to Hindu and Buddhist legends, spirits or divinities dwell in every outstanding feature of the landscape, be it a river, large tree, crossroads, cave, rock

The air is as pure as anywhere on Earth; the colours are dazzling in their intensity, and the altitude is intoxicating. A mountain wilderness opens up north and west of the Annapurna massif: Nye-Shang, gateway to the roof of Asia. The only sign of human habitation is the prayer flag – lung ta, 'wind horse' – fluttering in the breeze.

or lake. The soil itself has its own god, Bhumi.

None of this spares Nepali peasant farmers any of the crushing labour of their mountain homeland. In landscapes of gigantic dimensions, they exploit their land methodically and meticulously. Regularly each year, the monsoon rains sweep the topsoil into the valleys. Just as regularly, the farmers rebuild their terraces, repair their broken walls, and set about ploughing their tiny strips of earth – often so narrow that the oxen cannot turn the plough at the end of a row. In this stark, but majestic, environment, dominated by the still higher slopes and by similar terraces carved into the mountainsides opposite, the hill people eke out their lives.

Forests of *khasru* oaks cover the mountains' uncultivated areas, mostly the more arid, north-facing slopes. They provide one of the two major sources of fuel – along with dried cow dung. In among the oaks tree rhododendrons rise up to 65 feet, daubing the mountainsides between February and April with banks of red blossom – Nepal's national flower. Orchids flourish in the forests' humid depths – so many of them, in fact, that botanists still regularly discover hitherto unknown species. Among the most beautiful and best known is the white-flowering *coelogynes* which blossoms at the beginning of the hot season in April. In the higher altitudes, the *khasru* oaks give way to forests of pine, less varied in colour, though they too have their banks of rhododendrons, becoming paler and more stunted the higher you go. Reigning supreme among the pines is the majestic Himalayan cedar or deodar.

During the hot season, herdsmen climb the mountainsides to take up their quarters in *goths* or shelters in the forest clearings, while their animals graze above on the *lekhs* – mountain ridges low enough to lose their snow caps in summer. The vegetation on these is good for humans as well as animals and is rich in *dzari bhuti*, medicinal roots and herbs which villagers gather and sell for export. Occasionally – particularly in eastern Nepal – a visitor may catch a glimpse of the *danphe* or impeyan pheasant, a creature which far outstrips its European cousins for exotic colouring.

The herdsmen's charges consist mostly of goats and yaks (the huge oxen native to neighbouring Tibet) or, more commonly, yak half-breeds. Unlike the water buffaloes at lower altitudes, yaks can be mated with cows, the resulting half-breeds combining the yak's resistance to the cold with the cow's ability to survive on lower slopes. They make excellent pack animals and the females are good milk-producers.

Stark Himalayan slopes rise above Mustang in north-central Nepal. In the valley bottom, the autumn harvest of buckwheat has been gathered from the patchwork fields – it will later be mixed with millet to make the heavy porridge known as dhinro, *a staple in the diet of Nepal's higher regions. Districts such as Mustang lie in the rain shadow of the Annapurna massif and consequently rely on melting snows for their supplies of water.*

Brightly clad women gather the millet harvest in central Nepal. Millet is one of the most widely grown crops in the country. It is used in dhinro, *but also in various home-brewed alcoholic drinks, such as* jhanr *(a kind of beer),* tumba *(a weak beer popular with the Sherpas) and the spirit* raksi.

The valley of the dream

The lush green valley of Kathmandu is Nepal's spiritual as well as its geographical heart. It is the one place where the kingdom's different castes, tribes and religions can meet more or less on equal terms. It includes the great *stupa* (dome containing sacred relics) of Swayambhunath, the country's most important centre of Buddhist pilgrimage, rising from a small green hill west of the city of Kathmandu. To the east is the Hindu temple of Pashupatinath where the faithful gather from all over Nepal and India on cold nights in February or March to celebrate the festival of the god Shiva.

Dominating much of modern Kathmandu is the home of King Birenda. The kings of Nepal are traditionally regarded as incarnations of the Hindu god Vishnu.

The Valley (as it is usually known) has long been considered a tempting prize. In the 17th century it was famed for its beautiful cities and rich crops of chillies, sugar cane, ginger and turmeric, as well as its locally woven textiles. Its rulers, however, were divided among themselves and in the 18th century the Valley fell to Prithvi Narayan Shah, king of the tiny mountain realm of Gorkha to the west. He conquered Kathmandu in 1768; he also adopted the policy of shutting his country off from the outside world that lasted until the 1950s.

The blossom of the tree rhododendron is Nepal's national flower. The tree rhododendron – which can grow as high as 65 feet – is just one among a number of species of the plant that flourish in the country, depending on altitude and the orientation of the slopes. The more stunted, shrub-like varieties that grow higher up are those that are familiar to European garden lovers.

The impeyan pheasant or danphe *is the Nepali national bird. Its habitat is among the* lekhs *(mountain ranges without permanent snow) of western Nepal. The spirit-worshipping* jhankri *medicine men of parts of central Nepal like to wear headdresses of* danphe *feathers for their full-moon ceremonies.*

His descendants fell out with the British in India in 1814: the resulting war lasted two years and, at the end, the victorious British were so impressed by their opponents' mountain warriors from Gorkha that they recruited many of them into their own army, creating the famous Gurkha regiments.

A mythical story tells how the Valley was found, in the distant past, by the *bodhisattva* Manjushri (a *bodhisattva* is one who forswears the delights of the Buddhist state of blessedness, Nirvana, in order to lead others on the way to enlightenment). While meditating on a mountain in China, Manjushri dreamt of a lake surrounded by green hills. Rising from the centre of the lake was a huge and beautiful lotus flower, from which emanated a bright blue flame. The holy man recognised this as a manifestation of the Adi-Buddha or Swayambhu, the supreme being or Self-Existent One. Manjushri mounted his white she-lion and set off in search of the lake.

He found it in the valley of Kathmandu, which was then filled with water (modern geological research has shown that the valley was, indeed, once a lake). He paid homage to the divine flame and then decided that the place should be peopled. He drew his sword and sliced through the hills to the south, at the spot now known as the Chobar Gorge, to let the lake's waters out . . . which is how Nepal's sacred river, the Bagmati, was formed. The lake dried out and worshippers duly arrived, settled and multiplied. On the spot where the seed of the lotus plant had sprouted from the silt of the lake's floor, they built a temple to the goddess Gujeswari (a Hindu deity, but the boundaries between the two religions have always been fairly fluid in Nepal). On the spot where the plant blossomed on the surface of the water, they built the first temple of Swayambhunath.

If one is standing on a hill of the Valley's rim at sunrise on a winter morning, the legend does not seem far-fetched. Filling the Valley like a lake is the milky tide of the early morning mist, while rising from it, like Manjushri's lotus flower, is the gilded pinnacle of the present Swayambhunath *stupa*, glinting in the sun's first rays, with the painted eyes of 'Supreme Buddhahood' gleaming out beneath. The old tale seems to encapsulate a symbolic truth.

Mountains of divine majesty

If the lush green hills of the Kathmandu Valley represent the more smiling face of Nepal, the world's greatest mountain ranges offer a more fearsome aspect. The word *himalaya* means abode (*alaya*) of snow (*hima*) – it refers to everything that lies above the line of permanent snow, in other words everything over 18,000

A Sherpa man strikes up on a dramyen, *the stringed instrument of his people. The Tibetan New Year,* Lo Sar, *is the year's chief family festival, accompanied by dancing and singing. Although living within Nepal, the Sherpas belong by culture to Tibet: their religion is Tibetan Buddhism; their language is a Tibetan dialect; even their dress is Tibetan. The couple here are both wearing traditional costume – for the woman, a light-coloured silk undergarment, with a dark woollen dress over it and brightly striped front and back aprons.*

The mountain edges of the Kathmandu Valley rise behind the rooftops of Newari houses in Bhaktapur. The Newars usually build three-storeyed houses, the kitchen on the top floor running on to a roof terrace. This terrace is the family's inner sanctum; few outsiders are ever allowed on to it and certainly never anyone from a lower caste. Here, the women chat, enjoy the sun and get on with their daily tasks, which may include, as here, hanging out lengths of dyed cotton to dry.

A gaily painted balcony contrasts with the simple whitewash and shingle roof of a house high in the valleys of northern Nepal; it belongs to a lama (a priest of the Tibetan branch of Buddhism). Hanging from the roof is a yak's tail, for centuries a valuable commodity in the trade between Tibet, Nepal and India. The tails were used as fly whisks which, when attached to a silver handle, became a symbol of high rank: only kings and important civil and religious dignitaries were allowed to have them.

feet. This no man's land of ice and cold is the home of the (probably) mythical yeti, or abominable snowman. For Hindus, it also contains the mountain Gauri Shankar, home of Shiva and Parvati, his consort. Here, too, hermits withdraw to mortify the flesh and meditate, sheltering from the worst of the cold in caves and disciplining themselves with yoga, as taught by the example of Shiva himself.

The Himalayas have never formed an impassable barrier. Everest (lying on the frontier between Nepal and Tibet), Annapurna and the other great peaks have not prevented the people of the south-facing, Nepali slopes from sharing a common culture with those of the northern, Tibetan slopes. Nepal's various Bhotiya peoples living along the northern border (including, most famously, the Sherpas) are of Tibetan stock. For centuries, caravans of yaks, mules and foot-bearers have crossed and recrossed the Himalayan passes, carrying medicinal plants, salt and other minerals south from Tibet, and wheat, gemstones and silver north from Nepal and India. These processions – nowadays carrying produce such as paraffin – can still be seen winding their way through the high Kuti and Kyirong passes and, spectacularly, the Thorong La, offering some of the best views of Annapurna's north face.

In eastern Nepal, the country's northern border corresponds roughly with the ridge of the Himalayan range. West of Annapurna it bends northwards to encompass a region that has more in common with the highlands of Tibet than the rest of Nepal. Sheltered from the monsoon rains by the twin massifs of Annapurna and Dhaulagiri, districts such as Manang,

Mustang, Dolpo and Mugu rely on the melting snows of early summer for irrigation – producing surprisingly abundant harvests of barley, millet and buckwheat. Villages cling to the mountainsides, their cube-like mud and stone houses seemingly piled one on top of the other. Buddhist prayer flags flutter in the icy wind from their roofs, while only the village *gompa* (monastery) can be distinguished at a distance from the other buildings. Apart from the villages and their fields, a few gnarled juniper trees seem to be the only other living things in a landscape of rock and snow.

Patterns of village life

Outside north-western Nepal, most villages are more like scattered groups of hamlets, with (in the case of Hindu communities) different castes congregating in their own corner. Village lands often include some forest, a few areas of grazing land, some rocky or scrub wasteland, all held in common by the villagers, as well as the various family plots terraced into the mountain-sides. In lower altitudes where water for irrigation is plentiful, rice is the staple crop. Higher up, people grow maize, millet, barley and buckwheat. Farmhouses are built on the terraces beside the family land.

These houses, along with their farm buildings, are built around a courtyard, or *aangan*, with a wall at one end to keep out the larger livestock. There is usually a barn (where the young buffalo and cattle are kept at night), a straw stack, poles to hang drying maize cobs on, and a cage-like structure on stilts to store yams and

Spring in the high valleys. The patterns of the farming year vary with altitude. In the lower-lying areas, farmers expect to grow three crops each year; in the higher altitudes, they get only one. Rice grows at an altitude as high as 7000 feet. Above that, maize, millet, wheat and barley are grown in succeeding years. In the very highest cultivable valleys, the chief crops are barley, buckwheat and potatoes.

marrows out of the reach of nibbling animals. Most farms will have their own vegetable plots nearby, cultivating peppers, tomatoes, aubergines and sweet potatoes. Their fruit trees produce bananas, guavas, pawpaws, mangoes, persimmons, mandarins, lemons, pears and peaches, depending on the region.

Another standard item found near the house is a bamboo thicket. Bamboo is the most intensively used of all local materials. Herdsmen following their flocks in summer use bamboo mats to cover the mobile shelters they take with them like tents from place to place. Similar mats are rolled into tall cylinders and smeared with clay to make a kind of grain silo. The young shoots coming off the bamboo's main stem are woven into winnowing fans, sieves, baskets, cradles, bird traps, even muzzles for dogs. A bamboo stem chopped off beneath a knot becomes a bottle, bucket or churn. When

building a house, people used bamboo scaffolding to clamber up in order to slot the roof timbers in place and put on the roof itself. Bamboo also provides the uprights for the swings that village people erect throughout the country in the season between the family festival of Dasain in October and the five-day Festival of Lights, or Tihar, about a month later. Finally, bamboo shoots are widely used in cooking, adding a tangy flavour to even the blandest of dishes.

The courtyard in front of the house is where family members thresh, dry and winnow the harvests of rice, wheat and millet, and feed the goats and hens; weave their cotton and wool and the flax-like fibres of the ramie plant. It is where they make the rice-straw mats that everyone sits and sleeps on, and where the men make their bamboo winnowing fans. Visitors are welcomed in the courtyard, which is also where young

Fetching water from the nearest spring or well is a woman's job in Nepal. The purity of the water is important for ritual as well as hygienic reasons. Members of one caste will never share their water or food cooked in water with members of another caste.

mothers who have recently given birth relax after an invigorating mustard-oil massage. Here the women delouse one another and their children, while their babies sleep under cloth-covered bamboo tripods. Everyone foregathers in the courtyard for the afternoon snack of grilled soya seeds and citrus fruit seasoned (strangely to Western tastes) with salt and pepper. Members of the higher castes also have altars to Vishnu, the preserver of life, in their courtyards, with basil plants growing on either side of them.

The houses are generally rectangular, though some people in central Nepal live in oval dwellings. There are usually two storeys, with a verandah on the ground floor at the front. In the east of the country a wide balcony runs right around the house on the first floor.

Construction follows time-honoured patterns. Once the foundations have been laid and various religious rituals seen to, family and friends get to work raising the walls. These are made of local stone, bound together with the clayey earth of the mountain terraces mixed with water. At lower altitudes, a house's central pillars and main beams are all made from *sal* wood (notable for its supple strength), with chestnut used for less

important beams; higher up, pine and cedar are used. Windows are small with wooden shutters – glass is virtually unknown.

With the essentials of the house finished, the women start putting in the finishing touches – by no means a light task. They apply the final layer of protective cladding to the outside, paint the inside and level off the earth floor – this is later coated with a pungent mix of earth and cow dung. In the kitchen they build a raised area for storing water pitchers, the place for drying wood and the meat safe. Many of these are one-off jobs, but others need constant repair. The cladding on the outside is renewed each year during the festival of Dasain. The basic materials are lime and clay; the house may be whitewashed, or colourwashed brilliant shades of ochre yellow or red. In some regions, the women paint stylised patterns of flowers, leaves and animals on the walls.

Nepali houses do not have chimneys. The hearth, on which the cooking is done and around which the family gathers in the evenings, is simply a square-shaped trough dug into the earth floor. Cooking pots are held over the fire by resting them on three big stones or on a

Women winnow the paddy rice in a square in Bhaktapur in the Kathmandu Valley. During the harvest, all the town's squares become like farmyards as the crops are beaten, winnowed and dried. Presiding over the scene, meanwhile, is each square's shrine to the elephant-headed god of good fortune, Ganesh.

metal tripod. Sometimes there is also a crude oven, made from bricks or stones.

In the evenings, the father of an orthodox high-caste family sits to the right of the fire. He is joined there by any visitors, who sit nearer to or farther from him according to their rank. Members of the lowest *harijan* or untouchable castes have to sit in the courtyard or, possibly, on the verandah; they will certainly never be allowed to cross the threshold. Families from the highest, priestly caste, the Brahmans, often have a second hearth or even a separate building where members of lower castes can sit and be entertained – in this way, the family dwelling is left unsullied. Whatever the case, the atmosphere by the fire will be thick with smoke while the women of the house cook the *dhinro* for the evening meal. This is a thick porridge, which is mixed with chilli and vegetable soup to make the standard dish for the day's two main meals in families too poor to have rice every day – outside Nepal's lower-lying regions, rice is still something of a luxury.

Furniture is basic. A few straw mats and a wooden chest for storing clothes are normally the chief pieces. Apart from these, a family's most important possessions will be pots and pans made from copper or copper alloys. Cutlery is largely unknown since most people scoop up their food with their right hand. The exception is along Nepal's northern frontier where some women carry around with them a silver spoon decorated with turquoise and attached by a silver chain to their necklaces.

When eating – which is done sitting cross-legged on the floor – the main dish is served on a large platter or *thali*, with any accompaniments handed out in small copper bowls. People wash themselves carefully before the meal, and then, after it, rinse out their mouths. In between times, they will have been drinking out of a common jug but without letting it touch their lips. The

Nepalis have strict rules about hygiene, both ritual and literal. They would never, for example, touch any object regarded as *jutho*, or ritually unclean.

Running water is rare. As a result, water has to be collected and stored in large earthenware pitchers (*gagri*). These usually have narrow necks with splayed mouths, and are carried by resting the base on your hip and hugging the neck with your arm. A comfortable carrying position is important, because much of a woman's day will be spent going to and fro between her home and the nearest well or spring – which may be up to half-an-hour's walk away.

Among the Sherpas and other Bhotiya peoples of Nepal's northern lands, the ground floor of a house is given over to the livestock while the family live on the first floor, which is often divided into smaller rooms.

Wood sellers carry their wares through Durbar Square in Kathmandu. Wood is still the most widely used fuel in Nepal, even in the cities. As a result, forests are disappearing at an alarming rate – a problem that the government is now beginning to tackle.

Women in bright saris haggle with a street seller over some of the glass bracelets and bangles that are such beloved adornments. The tasselled red-and-black hanks of cloth hanging behind and to the right are another vital piece of attire. The women plait them into their pigtails to make them look thicker and more attractive.

These tend to be more heavily furnished than elsewhere in Nepal, with carved and painted dressers, low tables and the family altar elaborately carved. People sit and sleep on wooden platforms covered with warm, thick-piled carpets. The impression is cosy, with copperware, woodwork and carpets glowing in the firelight, a pot of salted tea brewing on its hob, all mingled with the smell of incense from the altar and the acrid odour of *ghee* (clarified butter) from the cooking area. Bhotiya homes are the only ones in Nepal equipped with an indoor privy. Some homes in the Mustang district have their own tiny chapels, adorned with frescoes and brightly painted wooden statues.

Muted echoes of the caravans

The homes of the Thakali people of Tukche, north of the Kathmandu Valley, are in a category of their own. Tukche lies in the valley of the Kali Gandaki (also known as the Thak Khola) where it slices between the massifs of Dhaulagiri and Annapurna, carving some of the deepest gorges on Earth. Every morning a fierce wind starts whistling up the valley from the south, to abate only at sunset. Sheltering from its swirling gusts, the richer Thakalis live in imposing houses with blank fronts, flat roofs and beautiful inner courtyards. For centuries, they have been known as the most

Using a yoke to carry things (including children) is common in the Kathmandu Valley and the lower-lying parts of Nepal. Higher up on the mountainsides, a large basket carried on the back with a head strap to hold it in place is more usual. It is an efficient way of carrying things, with the weight of the basket evenly distributed along the spine.

The period following childbirth is a time of unparalleled leisure for a Nepali woman. She is still ritually unclean, and as a result not allowed to take part in the household tasks. She devotes herself entirely to her baby, while the rest of the family look after her every need and feed her a succession of richly nourishing meals. During the colder days of winter, the mother and child are left to catch what warmth they can in the courtyard. The mother is massaged regularly with mustard oil, while the baby sleeps under a cloth-covered bamboo tripod.

entrepreneurial of the northern peoples, a reputation confirmed in the last century when they were given the monopoly of the salt trade with Tibet.

The great days of the old caravan trails were dealt a severe blow in 1950 when Communist China invaded Tibet. Although the Thakalis have diversified their trade into other areas, an air of decay clings to the mansions of the former merchant princes. Many families have transferred to more convenient, modern quarters in Kathmandu and elsewhere, leaving their mansions in the charge of bailiffs and a few ancient retainers. Outside in the streets, old women shuffle in threadbare velvet slippers from door to door, their faces hidden under voluminous shawls. The jingling train of a caravan, its mules decked out with headdresses of dyed-red yaks' tails, passes by, as resplendent as ever to the untrained eye of the outsider. But where it would once have been laden with the wealth of Tibet, it now carries rice and fertilisers from Pokhara in western Nepal north to Mustang.

The Newars of the Kathmandu Valley have a similar reputation to that of the Thakalis. They are renowned traders, though they boast a still more sophisticated cultural heritage. Their homes, clustering together in cities such as Kathmandu or Bhaktapur, often in what used to be Buddhist monasteries (*bahals*), are large brick buildings, with overhanging tiled roofs and windows sheltered by carved latticework grills. Newar architects are said to have invented the design of the pagoda and one of them, Arniko, is believed to have introduced it to the Chinese when invited to Peking by

The ten-day festival of Dasain in October is celebrated throughout Nepal. Events include animal sacrifices in honour of the goddess Durga on Durga Puja, the ninth day. Dasain is also a great family festival when everyone goes home to be with parents, brothers and sisters, and bamboo swings like this are erected outside villages for the enjoyment of the children.

the Emperor Kublai Khan. Certainly in the 13th century the Newars built the oldest and most beautiful palaces, pagodas and temples in the Kathmandu Valley, setting the dominant style for centuries to come.

Only in the mid-19th century did a new style of any importance emerge – that associated with the Rana family, who were Nepal's effective rulers for just under a century until 1951, governing in a strange relationship as hereditary prime ministers in the name of the king, but also taking to themselves the title of Maharajahs of Nepal. Under their influence, the prevailing style was based on the mock-Italianate of Victorian Britain, prompting many of Nepal's great families to remodel their ancient palaces.

Sherpas gather for the colourful Saturday market in their chief town Namche, not far from the foot of Everest. Their skills in negotiating the mountains – displayed most famously by Tenzing Norgay who accompanied Sir Edmund Hillary to the top of Everest in 1953 – mean that they are known worldwide as hardy mountain guides.

The Ranas were ousted after King Tribhuvan re-asserted his powers in 1951, but the marks left on the country by their free-spending, despotic period of rule are still there to be seen – not least in the Victorian palaces of the nobles. These are often slightly crumbling but have great charm; they are usually surrounded by parks full of the local flowering shrubs, as well as others that were among the Ranas' imports: jacarandas, bougainvilleas, magnolias and towering monkey puzzle trees. They add their touch of splendour to the flowered tapestry of the Kathmandu Valley in the period immediately preceding the monsoon season – the driest part of the year, when the air is thick with mosquitoes, and the stillness is broken only by rumbling forerunners of the storms to come.

The coming of the rains

The monsoon arrives around the middle of June. There is a violent thunderstorm, and then the rains set in. Every day they pour down for hours on end, especially in the evening and at night. Suddenly, all forms of animal and plant life seem to proliferate and grow at an extraordinary rate: grass, mildew, insects, grubs, mushrooms and funguses, lizards, spiders, weeds and frogs, whose constant croakings are among the most characteristic sounds of the monsoon.

The monsoon, bringing as it does 120-150 inches of rain annually, defines the seasons of the farming year. It is at its most intense from mid-June to mid-August; then it tails off until it dies away in mid-October. These four months are the busiest of the year for farmers, when the herds grazing the summer pastures of the high mountains produce most of the milk to be turned into cheese and butter, and when in the lowlands the rice seedlings have to be planted out during clear spells. Whole communities turn out for the rice planting because there is much to do – flooding the paddies, then ploughing and levelling them to receive the seedlings – if the harvest is to be ready by October or November.

After the rice harvest, the autumn wheat and barley are sown. The thick mists of winter will encourage their

A wayside seller offers piles of sindhur powder to pilgrims on their way to Pashupatinath, one of the most important of all temples dedicated to the god Shiva. Married women rub the powder (made from coloured dust mixed with mustard oil) into the partings in their hair; it is also rubbed into the foreheads of pilgrims returning from Pashupatinath.

Cotton carders ply their trade outside the Machhendranath Temple in Kathmandu. Originally from the Terai, the cotton carders – like most skilled workers in Nepal – form their own caste, in which the secrets of their trade are passed down from generation to generation. People give them raw or woven kapok cotton, which they then turn into mattresses, pillows and padded bedspreads. These carders are working on the so-called 'harps' they use to turn the cotton fibre into yarn.

The spectators alone are a colourful sight during the summer Indrajatra festival in Kathmandu's Durbar Square. One of the festival's highlights is the procession in which a specially chosen young girl, believed to be an incarnation of the goddess Taleju, is borne through the streets on a flower-decked chariot. With her are two young boys representing the gods Ganesh and Bhairav.

growth, and they will be harvested in the spring. During May, the rice is seeded on the lowlands, ready to be planted out when the monsoon comes round again, while higher up the farmers sow their maize. This will be reaped in July and August, to be replaced with millet, which is reaped in autumn.

In the religious calendar, the arrival of the monsoon corresponds to one of the year's more ominous periods. For the Hindus, this is the time of year when the gods take temporary leave of the Earth, and demonic forces are allowed free rein to harass humankind. Fortunately, the gods return in time for the festival of Janai Purnima, which falls in July or August depending on the cycle of the moon. During Janai Purnima, priests hand out bracelets of gold thread (*rikhi doro*) which are believed to ward off evil. After the tasks of the agricultural year, these festivals are one of the chief preoccupations of

many Nepalis. People joke that there are more festivals in Nepal than days of the year in which to celebrate them. Certainly, the Hindu religion seeps into every aspect of life. Many people still start and finish each day by making *puja* offerings of flowers, rice, incense and holy water to the gods. They arrange all these on copper platters and present them either at the local temple or in the *puja kotha*, a room set aside for the gods by those with large enough houses.

The year's festivals are also an excuse for a good time. Village people get together to sing and dance; street sellers do a brisk trade in *raksi* (a home-distilled spirit made from millet) and the weaker *jhanr* beer; families, or sometimes whole communities, head out into the countryside for picnics. Among the most spectacular festivals are those in which gods are dragged through the streets on chariots with solid wood wheels. One such festival in Kathmandu celebrates a goddess of flesh and blood, the *Kumari*. She is a young girl chosen, after a series of ordeals, from among the daughters of the Shakya caste of silver- and goldsmiths: these ordeals include being left alone in a darkened room with bloody buffalo heads – the girl must remain calm throughout. The *Kumari* is believed to be a human incarnation of the goddess Taleju and remains the *Kumari* until puberty, after which she retires into ordinary life and another girl is chosen to take her place.

Greatest of the festivals is Dasain, which lasts for ten days at the end of the monsoon season. Its theme is the restoration of order after a season of turbulence. This is when people renew the white- and colourwashing of their homes, and also when they buy new clothes. Dasain has the fearsome goddess Durga at its centre, representing the triumph of good over the forces of chaos. Starting on the seventh day of the festival, huge numbers of animals are sacrificed to her – no fewer than 108 buffaloes and 108 goats at one temple in Kathmandu. On the eighth and ninth days, sacrifices are made to invite blessings on all instruments of labour. Machines ranging from villagers' bicycles to aeroplanes sitting on the tarmac at Tribhuvan International Airport

A passer-by turns a prayer wheel on the outside of a Buddhist temple. Inside each wheel is a strip of paper with the words of a prayer inscribed on it. Individuals say their prayers, but the wheels are believed to have the effect of multiplying these prayers, and thus of helping the spiritual progress of humankind.

Nepal is officially a Hindu country, and the cow is as sacred there as in India. It provides such essential products as milk, cheese and butter, not to mention dung, used as both a fertiliser and a fuel. The cow is also believed to incarnate Lakshmi, consort of Vishnu and goddess of wealth. On the third day of the Festival of Lights, or Tihar, in November, all cows are washed and garlanded, as here.

are all sprinkled with blood. The armed forces make similar sacrifices so that their arms may be effective.

By the tenth and final day, order is believed to have been restored. Civil servants renew their oaths of allegiance to the King; children pay their respects to their parents, grandparents and other elders. In return, they receive dabs of vermilion paste, *tikas*, on their foreheads between the eyebrows. This is a sign of blessing, also dispensed by the *pujari* (priests of Hindu temples) when people leave their offerings. In fact, *tikas* have to some extent lost their religious significance nowadays, with some women wearing ones made from plastic rather than powder, and in different colours, according to what outfit they are wearing that day.

Generally speaking, the clothes that Nepali people wear conform to well-defined codes. For men, formal attire consists of the *daura-surwal* (a tunic and baggy, jodhpur-like trousers), with a Western-style jacket and a *topi*. The *topi* is a cap similar in style to those worn in India (often associated with the late Indian prime minister Jawaharlal Nehru), except taller and usually brightly coloured rather than white; Nepali men are not allowed to appear at official occasions without one.

The women are much more colourful, with a fondness for reds and pinks. In town, they wear saris over short-sleeved undergarments known as *cholos*, which are made of padded cotton in winter and lighter materials in summer. In the country, they wear a *phariya*, which differs from the sari in that it is not folded back over the shoulder. It is held in place with a *patuka*, a long piece of unbleached cotton wrapped around the waist, with pleats at the front that can hold keys, purses, or even picnic lunches when going out to work in the fields all day. In winter, better-off women keep themselves warm with *pashmina* (cashmere) shawls.

Tears for the bride

Traditional marriages and their attendant ceremonies are still the norm in Nepal. For the bride, dressed in red sari and veil, her wedding day is the greatest day of her life. Not that she will have had much choice in the matter. Marriages are arranged by parents, always between families of the same caste. For both families, they are an opportunity for lavish show, the propitious day and time having been fixed by a Brahman astrologer after

A body is burnt at Pashupatinath. Its ashes will then be borne by the sacred river Bagmati until they reach the Ganges on the plains far below. For Hindu funerals, the bodies of women are wrapped in yellow or red shrouds, the bodies of men in white ones. While in mourning the family of the dead person are temporarily 'unclean', and have to undergo a period of strict fasting. It is the task of the dead person's eldest son to set light to the funeral pyre.

examining the horoscopes of the bridal pair.

For the ceremony, an altar with a burning fire in it is set up in the courtyard of the bride's home. One of the key moments comes when the groom casts an offering into the sacrificial flame – at that point he is believed to pass from one stage of his existence to the next: he has become the head of a household. Later, bride and groom are tied together with a shawl and go round and round the fire seven times – they are now considered to be united. The next great moment comes when the groom carries his bride away from her family home. She sighs and weeps – as is customary – while a litter or carriage bears them to the home of the groom's parents. Following them are their family and friends; preceding them are musicians playing the haunting melodies of a traditional fanfare. Women's movements have yet to make much impact in Nepal, and from the time of her marriage onwards a woman is completely bound to her husband. Even after his death, it is not normal for her to remarry – though the old custom of *sati*, when the widow burnt herself alive on her husband's funeral pyre, has long since passed away.

Funerals are relatively simple affairs. A few hours after a person dies his or her body is taken down to a riverside *masan ghat*, a place reserved for cremations, and laid on a stretcher. It is then wrapped in a shroud – white for men, red or yellow for women – and burnt. In Kathmandu, when people feel the end approaching, they ask to be taken to Pashupatinath on the banks of the Bagmati, which is considered a propitious place to die. The dead person's eldest son sets light to the pyre. If the dead person was a married man, his widow casts off all her jewellery – she will never wear it again – and from then on will wear only white.

Mourning lasts 13 days, during which the family observe a strict fast. At the end of the 13 days, they and their home are ritually purified, since those in mourning are believed to be unclean. Further rituals expel the soul of the deceased, to prevent it from haunting the place.

These are the Hindu rituals of Nepal's majority. For the Buddhists, especially those of Tibetan stock in the north, things are different. Many of them bury their dead, though nowadays some are adopting the Hindu practice of cremation. In the north, it is customary for a *lama* (a priest of the Tibetan branch of Buddhism) to come and read from the ancient Book of the Dead every day for 49 days – this helps to guide the dead person's soul on the perilous journey to its next incarnation. In the far north-west of the country, some people still follow the Tibetan custom of cutting up the body and then leaving it on the mountaintops for crows and vultures to devour.

Caste skills in the crafts

Hinduism is Nepal's official religion – so it is not surprising that the caste system is so entrenched. The numerous castes correspond to different trades and crafts. People are blacksmiths, gold- and silversmiths, brass or bronze workers, tailors, minstrels, street-sweepers, potters, butchers, gardeners and so on, simply because they were born into the appropriate caste, rather

A young bride, with eyes downcast under her traditional red veil, prepares for her marriage. Women do not inherit wealth in Nepal, but on their wedding day they receive substantial dowries – furniture, jewels, clothes and cash.

A Nepali widow is no longer expected to burn herself on her husband's funeral pyre. Even so, the consequences of widowhood are fairly drastic. The woman takes off all her jewellery, breaks her glass bracelets, lets her hair hang loose and no longer bothers to rub sindhur powder into her parting – she also dresses in white from now on. She is regarded as ritually unclean and strictly speaking is not allowed to marry again.

than through any preference of their own. Their only choice is between working the land or practising the craft of their caste, or combining both.

The caste system may impose something of a straitjacket, but it also concentrates the skills of Nepal's craftspeople. Visitors are struck by the variety and high standards of their work, especially that of the Newars, with their characteristic paintings and bronze statues of Hindu and Buddhist divinities.

One of the best places to see these crafts is a Buddhist rather than a Hindu place of worship: Bodhnath in the Kathmandu Valley, the most important centre of pilgrimage for the country's Tibetan Buddhists. Every winter, while their Himalayan villages are blanketed in snow, they converge on Bodhnath to pay homage to the Buddha and do the rounds of the

great *stupa* there – Nepal's largest. They count the beads on their rosaries and turn the prayer mills on the *stupa*'s outside wall, all the time chanting the sacred words of the mantra: *Om mani padme hum*. But if the sacred is all-important at Bodhnath, mammon too has its place. Shops and stalls around the *stupa*'s precinct are manned by Tibetan, Sherpa and other vendors, selling blankets, rugs and carpets woven in the mountains, lengths of cotton, jewellery, as well as religious objects. The Newars, too, are present, selling their statues.

The technique they use for making these is extremely ancient – it is another of the skills that Arniko is said to have taught the Chinese. First, the sculptor makes a wax model of his statue. Next, he covers it with an earthenware mould, which takes the shape of the wax model. He heats the whole thing, until the wax inside melts and drains out through a hole in the bottom. He uses the same hole to pour in molten metal. Then he leaves it to cool, and finally breaks the mould and polishes the statue, applying any finishing touches. Every statue made in this way is, of course, unique.

The gods are also sometimes represented with papier-mâché masks. Every year, masked performers dance through the streets and squares of Bhaktapur and old Kathmandu, re-enacting the titanic struggles between the forces of good and evil in the universe. In a way, these mystery cycles are also symbolic of Nepal and the Nepalis: their constant and unyielding struggle with nature at its most majestic, but also its harshest; their courage, their flair and their sheer doggedness.

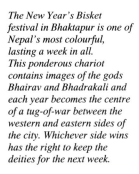

The unusual shape of the Nepali flag is based on that of the tribal flags of old. Red is the national colour, and the moon (Chandra) *and sun* (Surya) *are the emblems of the ruling Shah dynasty.*

The New Year's Bisket festival in Bhaktapur is one of Nepal's most colourful, lasting a week in all. This ponderous chariot contains images of the gods Bhairav and Bhadrakali and each year becomes the centre of a tug-of-war between the western and eastern sides of the city. Whichever side wins has the right to keep the deities for the next week.

Sri Lanka

When Adam and Eve were cast out of the Garden of Eden, they
sought refuge in Sri Lanka because it reminded them of their
former paradise – so runs an ancient legend which proves that the
beauties of this island have long been appreciated. Deserted
beaches bathed by the Indian Ocean, the jungle-festooned ruins of
former royal capitals, wild animals living freely in huge reserves
. . . Sri Lanka lacks nothing to make it an earthly paradise. But it
is more than that. It is a country where a particularly attractive
form of Buddhism pervades everything: the shape of the
landscape as well as the ways of living.

Previous page:
*A tea picker gathers the
tender young shoots that will
later go through a complicated
process of drying, sorting and
fermenting to become what is
still known as Ceylon tea.
The British first started
growing tea in Sri Lanka
(then known as Ceylon) in the
late 19th century. The crop
flourished and is now the
island's principal export –
it produces nearly 440 million
pounds a year.*

*The majestic sweep of the
palm alley dwarfs visitors to
the Royal Botanical Gardens
at Peradeniya near Kandy,
the former royal capital high
in Sri Lanka's central uplands.
The gardens cover more than
150 acres and are among the
most beautiful in Asia.
Among their other glories are
exotic arrays of orchids.*

*Exotic plants and flowers
abound in Sri Lanka, growing
wild throughout the island.
The most colourful grow in
the south-west, where the
climate is hot and humid.
In the drier east, jungles of
low bush and shrubs tend
to dominate.*

Island of Natural Splendour

The name Sri Lanka means 'resplendent land', and it is certainly appropriate for this emerald gem of an island set in the vivid blue of the Indian Ocean. In spite of the civil conflict which has torn parts of the country asunder over the last decade or so, Sri Lanka remains a place of charm and beauty. Outside the troubled regions, mostly in the north, island life carries on at its own deliberate pace, much as it has done for centuries. Old and new jog along together with disarming ease as ancient folk traditions and crafts handed down over countless generations flourish alongside a more modern economy based on the export of tea, rubber, coconut products, rice and sea food. The island's other great glory, its scenery and wildlife, has also survived the centuries remarkably unspoiled, and is protected by the authorities. It too has its economic place, as a lure to tourism, which has grown substantially since independence from Britain in 1948, and which continues despite the recent troubles.

The most striking thing about Sri Lanka's scenery is its diversity – all the more surprising in a region where nature is more notable for its scale than its variety: in the mountain ranges of northern India, for example, or the forests of Indonesia. In Sri Lanka, samples of many of the world's landscapes seem to have been bundled up together in the space of one island a little smaller in area than the Republic of Ireland. Among these, the three most important are the barren, largely rainless regions of the north and east, the highlands of the centre and the hot, humid regions of the south-west.

In spite of being so small, Sri Lanka also varies in climate as well as scenery. The only part to be lashed by the summer monsoon winds and their accompanying heavy rains is the south-west. The north and east get only light and unreliable rains for a few weeks between November and January. Temperatures vary comparatively little in a country so close to the Equator: between 23° and 31°C (73° and 88°F) along the coasts and on the inland plains; and between 14° and 24°C (57° and 75°F) in the highlands of the centre. It is rainfall, rather than temperature, however, which differentiates the various parts of the island and the kinds of vegetation that grow in them.

Poinsettias grow all over the hills and valleys of Sri Lanka's hot outer rim. In the centre of the island and in the highlands of the south, tropical vegetation gives way to a more temperate landscape: forests of conifers; bleak and windswept moorlands; crystal-clear streams tumbling through meadows grazed by cows that were originally imported from Holland or New Zealand.

Peacocks add yet another touch of the exotic to Sri Lanka. They seem to roam around everywhere: in the courtyards of houses, in the forests, and in the various nature reserves. The island is, in fact, a sanctuary for numerous animals – deer, boars, buffaloes as well as countless species of birds. The authorities are careful to protect rare species and have won international respect for their nature conservation policies.

The region around Jaffna is the heart of the arid north. Here, drought rules for at least six months of the year. Plains cracked by the lack of rain spread out for miles on end, covered with sparse, yellowing grass and dotted with clusters of coconut palms. This pattern continues down the east coast as far as Trincomalee and beyond to Batticaloa. Climbing slowly towards the centre of the island, the barren wastes of the north give way to a thick, scrubby undergrowth. This in turn yields

Kasyapa had been guilty of killing his father in order to gain the throne and tried to make amends by protecting artists and the Buddhist religion. It did him little good; he perished at the foot of this very rock in a battle against an army led by his brother.

Nowadays, only the ruins of his palace are left, but the splendour of the setting remains. Washing against the rock on all sides is a great sea of green: stretches of forest interspersed with rice paddies. In the distance rise

Sri Lankans were using vessels like these long before modern yachtsmen invented the catamaran. They are made by specialised local builders who use techniques that have existed for centuries. They are sturdy craft, despite their frail appearance, and can survive at sea in the roughest conditions. Most are fishing boats, coming back at the end of a good day with heavy cargoes of tuna and shark.

to steamy forests around Anuradhapura, Sigiriya and Polonnaruwa, three of Sri Lanka's former royal capitals.

This is the region of Rajarata, the 'land of the kings', where the island's first inhabitants, the Veddas, established themselves after arriving from the Indian mainland around 3000 BC. Many centuries later the Veddas were overrun by Sinhalese conquerors, who came by sea from northern India and also settled here, bringing their Buddhist religion with them and building their own impressive civilisation. One of the most remarkable surviving monuments to this is the great crag of Sigiriya, rising abruptly from a forest-covered plain. Here, in the 5th century AD, the mad king Kasyapa built a sumptuous palace of immaculate white stone, which, according to chroniclers of the period, seemed from the distance to float magically in the air.

the outer ramparts of the central highlands. It is a wild and lonely landscape, for despite the region's importance in the time of Kasyapa and before, later generations moved to Sri Lanka's lusher central and western parts. As a result Rajarata became a jungle wilderness, the haunt of elephants, buffaloes, leopards and monkeys. Only in recent years have the authorities started to encourage people to settle in the area once more. New villages have been built along with irrigation systems to bring in much-needed water. At the same time, the various Sinhalese remains, such as Kasyapa's palace, have been lovingly restored and preserved.

One of the factors which forced the Sinhalese to leave Rajarata was the pressure from a new wave of invaders: Hindu Tamils from southern India who had been raiding Sri Lanka since the 11th century and establishing themselves in the north of the island. Friction between these two races has continued down the centuries and is the cause of today's problems. Under the British, the Tamils, although a minority, held the majority of responsible white-collar jobs, but since independence the Sinhalese majority has reclaimed the top jobs. Both communities are well educated – Sri Lanka has the highest literacy rate (over 80 per cent) of any Asian country except Japan – and the Sinhalese feel that they have simply redressed an imbalance. The Tamils argue that they are being discriminated against. What began in the 1970s as a non-violent campaign against discrimination has escalated into a bloody guerrilla fight for an independent Tamil homeland in the north and east.

The difference between the prosperous south-west – rarely touched by the guerrilla violence – and the rest of the country is immediately apparent. From the western coastal city of Negombo (lying to the north of the capital Colombo) as far round as Hambantota on the south coast, the vegetation is noticeably more luxuriant than in the rest of the island. Dense plantations of coconut palms rise from the white sandy shores of narrow sea creeks; terraced rice paddies stretch inland, sparkling with countless shades of green. Irrigation channels pass through the undergrowth, with children and buffaloes wallowing in their cool depths, while houses shelter behind screens of brightly flowering shrubs. This is the most densely populated, as well as the richest, part of Sri Lanka. And it only comes to an end beyond Hambantota, in the region of Ruhuna. Here, suddenly, the luxuriance of Asia gives way to open bushland more reminiscent of Africa. This is especially true of the Yala National Park, where buffalo and wild elephants roam through the low scrub, while crocodiles drowse on the banks of ponds and small lakes.

Steam-powered traction vehicles can still sometimes be seen on the streets of Colombo, Sri Lanka's capital and busiest port. The city is an impressive, bustling place with numerous fine avenues and parks, Hindu and Buddhist temples, as well as some newer skyscrapers. It is famous for its bazaars and gemstone markets, but also has some appalling shanty towns around its edges.

Fishermen sort the catch at Kalkudah near Batticaloa on the east coast. To catch small fish like these, they use special shore nets. They simply throw the nets out to sea – having first anchored one end to the beach. Then they draw the nets back in, loaded with fish.

Sri Lankan children are adept at another, intriguing method of fishing. Perched on poles in the water, they cast out their lines to catch small fish feeding close to the shore. They rarely fall into the water and usually manage to go home with a good catch.

The south-west is undoubtedly Sri Lanka at its most open and welcoming, which is probably why so many generations of Western traders and colonisers were drawn to it: the Portuguese first, then the Dutch after 1658, and finally the British, who seized the island (then known as Ceylon) in 1796. All left their mark, but none more so than the British. The Portuguese and Dutch were above all interested in spices – and, to some extent, conversions to Christianity. But the British, arriving at a time when Western economic theories were more fully developed, set about exploiting the island's resources. They introduced the plantation system and transformed the economy. They were also the first Westerners to bring the whole island under their control. In 1815, after a long siege, they conquered the last bastion of Sinhalese independence, the kingdom of Kandy in the highlands north-east of Colombo.

These central highlands present yet another face of Sri Lanka. To the north, the city of Kandy is still the island's Buddhist capital, famous for its Temple of the Sacred Tooth. This houses the Sinhalese people's most ancient and sacred relic: what is believed to be a tooth of Siddhartha Gautama, who founded Buddhism in the 6th century BC. In the days of the kingdom of Kandy, possession of the tooth was believed to bestow legitimacy on the sovereigns, whose former royal palace

Until comparatively recent times, elephants were the principal beast of burden in much of Sri Lanka. Their role is less important nowadays, but they are still treasured by many country people. Some roam freely, especially in the nature reserves at Yala. Others are still used for various agricultural tasks. The ritual of the daily bath is ample proof of how much their owners continue to value the huge beasts.

still stands next door to the temple. Today, Kandy is a centre of pilgrimage for more than just Buddhists. The Temple of the Tooth is visited by thousands of tourists every year, while the city has been a favourite retreat from the heat of the plains ever since the British started using it as their chief summer hill station. It is also an important intellectual centre with one of the country's most highly regarded universities.

The hills surrounding Kandy are mostly open and rolling. Here, Sri Lanka's most important crop, tea, reigns supreme. Evergreen tea bushes cover whole hillsides, with the brightly coloured figures of pickers in brilliant saris moving constantly among them. To the south, the countryside grows wilder and more rugged as it rises to the highlands' second city, Nuwara Eliya. Roads weave through the hills, while in among the tea plantations on either side are small market gardens growing cabbages, lettuces, potatoes, carrots, leeks and turnips.

Nuwara Eliya was another hill station and preserves some fine specimens of British colonial architecture. But the region's affinity with Europe goes deeper than that. On either side of the city rise the mountains some travellers have called the 'Switzerland of Asia'. On their slopes are meadows grazed by cattle imported from Holland and New Zealand – the authorities have set up pilot farms to encourage locals to raise livestock. Farther still into the mountains, you reach Horton Plains where a landscape worthy of Scotland opens up on either side: huge expanses of moorland, streams rushing through the high grass, spinneys of gnarled trees . . . above all, an almost tangible stillness in a place rarely visited by either Sri Lankans or tourists.

Having reached Horton Plains, you begin to appreciate both the diversity and coherence of Sri Lanka. It is the rains that fall around Nuwara Eliya that feed the rivers and provide irrigation for the drier regions. Similarly, the prosperity of the west coast generates the means to exploit the country's resources effectively. Sri Lanka's contrasting elements all have their place in the whole.

Town and country

The Sri Lankans are not city-dwellers by and large. The majority live in the country, and most of the cities that do exist, such as Kandy, feel more like large market towns – they have none of the thronging density of people that strikes visitors to Indian cities. The two exceptions to this rule are Colombo on the west coast and Trincomalee on the east.

Colombo is first and foremost a port, founded by Arab traders as a staging post on the way to the Far East. Later, the Portuguese, Dutch and above all the British, each in their turn, spotted its strategic value, transforming it into one of the busiest ports on the trade routes between East and West. Today, it is a sprawling mass of more than half a million people, which still handles 90 per cent of Sri Lanka's overseas trade. It is also the capital, with all the commercial and political

Fish, along with rice, is one of the staples of the Sri Lankan diet. Here as on the Indian sub-continent, fish and meat alike are made into curries, with small red chillies as one of the favourite spices.

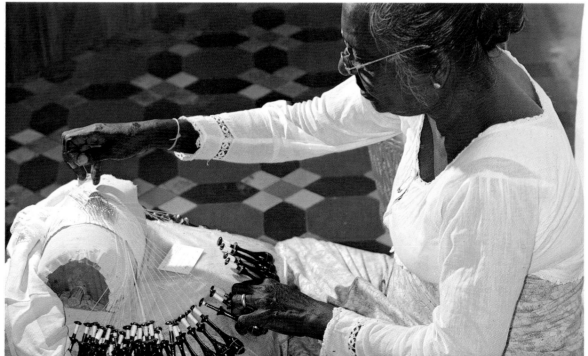

A lacemaker plies her trade in the region around Galle in the south. A variety of foreign influences have left their mark on Galle. Arab and Chinese navigators visited the harbour in ancient times, to be followed later by the Portuguese, who gave it its name. Then came the Dutch, who made it one of their trading bases and, for a time, the busiest port on the island.

Nearly a million pilgrims pour into the village of Kataragama every year for a ten-day festival in honour of the Hindu god of the same name. According to Hindu mythology, the warlike Kataragama is the second son of Siva and a powerful influence among the gods, well worth propitiating with elaborate rituals and sacrifices.

bustle, as well as some fine architecture, to go with that status. At its centre, the district known as the Fort – after a Dutch fort that once stood there – is the nation's administrative and business heart, with the presidential residence (a colonnaded structure in the finest British colonial style) and a varied collection of colonial and more modern office blocks housing government ministries, banks and the headquarters of the island's principal companies.

East of the Fort, the Pettah district is the city's chief shopping area. Narrow, dusty streets are lined with low, one- or two-storey houses which each have a garage-like opening at the front. This is where the shop-owners preside over their tumbling arrays of goods. South of the Fort, Colombo sprawls out along the sea front, merging with a number of once separate towns, such as Wellawatta, Dehiwala and Mount Lavinia.

In the east, Trincomalee has always been valued as a naval rather than a commercial port. At various points in its history it has been used by the Portuguese, Dutch, French, British as well as Sri Lankan navies. Nowadays, Trincomalee has much in common with other cities of the developing world: appalling poverty and shanty towns of flimsy structures made from planks, corrugated iron and bits of scrap. Only a few remains, such as those of a Portuguese fort rising from the promontory that dominates the harbour, remind the visitor of the city's former importance. A Hindu temple, also on the promontory, was built to replace an earlier temple destroyed by the Portuguese in a fit of missionary zeal in 1622; the remains of the old temple can still be seen rising from the bed of the Indian Ocean at the foot of a cliff nearby.

Sri Lankans are not, on the whole, fond of living in big, collective groups. Even in Colombo, homes tend to be low and reasonably spread out, and the same holds true in the countryside. Most country people like to live on their own patch of ground, with the result that the rural population is evenly distributed across the island. With the exception of the sparsely populated north and east, houses are dotted everywhere: at the sides of roads,

One young worshipper at the Kataragama festival holds a votive bunch of greenery. The Hindu Tamils started arriving in Sri Lanka from southern India in the 11th century, and they are still mostly concentrated in the north of the island, with Jaffna as their chief city. The other dominant ethnic group, the Buddhist Sinhalese, came from northern India around 600 BC. They are strongest in the south and west.

rising behind beaches, tucked away among rice paddies or coconut plantations. Most of these are simple affairs. Walls are made from baked mud, while a few plaited palm leaves provide the roof. Inside, there are rarely more than two rooms. Few houses have electricity or running water, and fetching water from the nearest well or stream is an important daily task, usually given to the women or children.

Scattered among these settlements are small market towns, where the country people sell their produce and buy items of hardware and the like. Most are lively, colourful places, with a constant flow of people in the market and around the bus stop – the bus is still the most common way for ordinary people to get around Sri Lanka. Among the houses lining the few streets, those belonging to local merchants, lawyers and doctors are not hard to spot, especially as they are often painted in gaudy shades of yellow, green, pink or red. To own a

Pilgrims at Kataragama are prepared to go to extraordinary lengths to prove their devotion to the god. At the simplest level, they offer him flowers and burn oil in his honour. But many also practise gruesome mortifications. Some roll in the dust around the temple and pierce their lips and cheeks with silver needles. Others go even further. Using hooks attached to their flesh, they pull small carts bearing an effigy of Kataragama through the streets. Or, as here, they use the hooks to suspend themselves painfully from a metal frame.

house like this is a sign of wealth and respectability, since it is built from stone or concrete, rather than mud and palm thatch.

Sri Lanka is dotted with numerous traces of colonial times. Rising from the hillsides are the stone plantation houses built by the British, often flanked by wide verandahs with porticoed flights of steps leading up to them. On the west coast, especially around Negombo, you can still find a few Portuguese-style houses and small churches.

Sri Lanka's chief Buddhist pilgrimage – the Esala Perahera – takes place in the old royal capital, Kandy every August. The highlight of the festival is when a magnificently caparisoned elephant processes through the streets bearing on its back the island's holiest Buddhist relic: a tooth believed to be from the Buddha himself.

Elephants decked in gold

The Sri Lankans are among the most fervently religious of Asian peoples. While many other countries in the region have been drawn by the tenets of socialist atheism or capitalist materialism, Sri Lanka has remained faithful to its ancient gods. The yearly round of religious festivals looms large in the imagination of most people, and more regular acts of devotion are common – many people, for instance, take daily offerings of lotus flowers, fruit or small strips of cloth to their nearest Buddhist shrine. Remarkably, this religious zeal has not, on the whole, bred intolerance. The Buddhists account for nearly 70 per cent of the population, but there are also thriving Muslim and Christian communities as well as the Hindus, all of whom are free to practise their faiths. Indeed, the dividing line between Buddhist and Hindu practices is often blurred – it is not uncommon for a Buddhist to take offerings to a Hindu shrine.

Testifying to this religious devotion are the numerous temples that dot the island. Among these, the Buddhist ones can easily be distinguished by their bell-shaped domes, or *dagobas,* rising above the trees and fields like the bodily presence of the Buddha himself. The Hindu temples tend to be more ornate, with contorted figures of their gods carved on their stone fronts and painted in brilliant colours. The great annual pilgrimages give people a special opportunity to express their fervour. Of these, the most spectacular are undoubtedly those taking place at Kandy, at Adam's Peak on the south-western edge of the central highlands and at Kataragama on the plains of the south-east.

Kandy's great pilgrimage is the procession known as the Esala Perahera which takes place each August. This is the one moment in the year when the chief priest at the Temple of the Sacred Tooth reveals the precious relic – normally kept concealed in a seven-layered, jewel-encrusted casket – to the eyes of the faithful. The whole event is one of extraordinary magnificence and display. The tooth is carried through the streets by a procession of elephants decked with rich brocades and fabrics made from thread of gold; on either side, troupes of musicians and dancers perform before the crowds in honour of the occasion. On the day of the festival people will pour into Kandy not only from the surrounding district but from the whole of the island – for many Sinhalese, indeed, it is a patriotic as well as a religious festival in which they celebrate their national culture.

The Pilgrimage of Suffering at Adam's Peak takes place in a more contemplative spirit. As with the Esala, it is a popular event with thousands of pilgrims converging on the mountain each year from the four corners of the island. But here the devotion required is rather more arduous. As night falls on the chosen day, the pilgrims set out up the mountain's sides. The climb to the 7359-foot summit is long and painful, and for some it all becomes too much. They collapse at the wayside, begging the Buddha to give them the strength to carry on. At the summit, they kneel in a small temple carved out of the rock, which shelters what is believed

A Buddhist dignitary bears all the finery of his office – as well as a more prosaic umbrella in case of rain – during the Esala Perahera festival. Until 1815, when the British overthrew the last Sinhalese king reigning in Kandy, it would have been the monarch himself who led the procession. Possession of the Buddha's tooth was highly important to the kings – they believed it was a symbol of divine favour for their rule.

to be an imprint of the Buddha's foot. Then, as dawn begins to break, the pilgrims turn their eyes to the east and watch in meditative silence as the sun emerges from behind a ridge of mountains. Finally, when the sun is clear of the peaks, they set off down the mountainside and back home.

The festival at Kataragama is different again. In the first place, it is a Hindu celebration – which does not, however, prevent many Buddhists from taking part. It also prompts acts of devotion and self-mortification that, to Western eyes at least, can seem decidedly extravagant. Some of the faithful, for example, drive nails and needles into their bodies; others go to the length of suspending themselves from iron hooks attached to their bare flesh.

Acts like these may seem gruesome to the outsider, but for the Sri Lankans they are a normal expression of faith. They may have their roots in the Hindu religion, but also fit well with the Buddhist desire for detachment from material things. And the influence of this desire is noticeable in Sri Lanka. Whilst few people are prepared to torture their bodies in order to reach the state of perfection, the Sri Lankans do not share the modern frenzy for consumer goods and riches that is common among many of their neighbours. Equally, you find a much greater loyalty to traditional values, especially those associated with the family: respect for one's elders and so on.

Tea, coconuts and a tradition of crafts

Sri Lanka still lives largely by the produce of land and sea. The largest number of jobs on the island owe their existence to the cultivation of tea, rice, coconuts and rubber, as well as to fishing. Of these, tea is easily the most important. Ceylon tea – it is still known by the

A group of tea pickers form a brightly coloured throng among the fields of a plantation. Tea is Sri Lanka's gold, bringing in more than half the country's export earnings. Not surprisingly, picking and then treating it are all done with the utmost care. The whole process also helps to employ several thousands of young Sri Lankans every year.

island's old name – is reckoned by many experts to be among the best in the world. The island produces well over 2.5 million tons of it every year, making tea its biggest export earner. In the central highlands, the tea plantations keep most of the population in work. They employ large numbers of pickers – going out every day, with baskets on their backs, to gather the few tender green leaves at the top of each bush – as well as general workers, who supervise the drying and processing of the picked leaves.

The coconut industry is also a good source of employment. Roughly a quarter of Sri Lanka's cultivable land is given over to coconut plantations, which between them produce more than 22,000 million nuts a year. One of their beauties is that they are so versatile, and hence sustain numerous different crafts and livelihoods. Among their various products are coconut oil, copra (used in cosmetics and some processed foods) and coir (the fibres of the husk, used in textiles and matting). The shell can also be turned into a fuel similar to charcoal, while an alcoholic syrup called *toddy* is made from the sap. To seek this sap out, men scramble up the trunk of a palm until they reach the very top, and then swing Tarzan-like from tree to tree using ropes slung between them.

All along the west and south coasts and on the east coast between Trincomalee and Batticaloa, small fishing villages cluster among the coconut palms lining the edges of beaches. Their methods are frequently primitive – though fairly effective as well. At Weligama near the island's southern tip, for example, the locals fish from the top of wooden poles which they stick into the sand a few yards out from the shore. Elsewhere, the fishermen take their nets and head out a short distance to sea in canoes made from hollowed-out palm trunks. They then drop the nets and return to shore. After a few hours they gently drag the nets – by now, with any luck, well laden with fish – back towards the beach, singing folk songs to keep their spirits up.

Negombo is one place where the fishermen actually spend time at sea. Their curious-looking, square-rigged boats are said to have given Western yacht designers the idea for the catamaran – they are certainly sturdy craft, able to stay out in most weathers. Each morning,

Once picked, the tea leaves are taken to the factory to be processed into the substance that most outsiders recognise as tea. They are first 'withered' (spread out on racks so that the moisture in them evaporates), rolled and sifted. They are then spread out in a cool, damp place to ferment. Finally, they are dried again and sorted (as here) into their various grades. The biggest buyers of the finished product are, of course, the British.

Tea bushes have to be carefully tended. They are pruned every year and cut right back every three years. Since they are evergreen plants, picking carries on throughout the year. Every fortnight, the pickers go round gathering the two youngest leaves on each plant and the bud, which is where the aroma is concentrated. The commonest variety of tea from Sri Lanka is Orange Pekoe.

Another flourishing industry in Sri Lanka is making batiks, which women like to wear on special occasions. To make them, the cloth – which starts off-white – is first starched, left to dry and then pounded with a stick to soften it up again. Next, the design is copied on to the material with a pencil. The cloth is then dipped in a succession of dyes, with different parts of the design masked in paraffin wax each time, to create the desired pattern of colours.

Every country has its Eldorado, and Sri Lanka is no exception. In Sri Lanka, in fact, the hope of finding hidden treasure is rather better founded than in many places. The island boasts rich seams of various precious and semi-precious stones, notably in the region around Ratnapura on the edge of the central highlands. The 'mines' here are distinctly rudimentary – little more than muddy water holes where men poke around for days on end to find a few stones that they will then sell on to local merchants.

One jewel-hunter sifts through his basket of spoils, while another looks on. Tourism has given a new boost to the industry by opening up a huge new market. The stones most commonly found are moonstones, garnets, cornelians, amethysts, aquamarines, zircons, sapphires and rubies. Needless to say, the authorities try to keep a tight rein on the whole business and impose a series of regulations. None the less, some 'mines' escape their attention and carry on a more profitable, illicit trade.

small fleets of them take advantage of the land breeze to head out for the well-stocked waters of the Gulf of Mannar, between Sri Lanka and India's southern tip. Later, the afternoon sea breeze sends them back in again. After that, in Negombo as elsewhere, the task is to sell their fish. This is not usually too difficult. Fish is one of the staples of the Sri Lankan diet, and fish markets are invariably the liveliest places in coastal villages, offering everything from lobster to shark meat to tuna.

All these activities tend to be carried out on an intimate scale. Wherever you go in Sri Lanka, you come across people working busily in small groups or workshops: a woman and her children making string from coconut fibre; a blacksmith hammering away in his smithy; carpenters and joiners out in a field sawing up a tree; a farmer, up to his calves in water, following a pair of buffaloes as he prepares a rice paddy for sowing. By and large, the same also holds true in the towns and cities. Everyone likes to have his own business, whether it is the street trader selling a few fruits laid out on a piece of newspaper on the pavement or the more prosperous tradesman selling meat and vegetables in his own shop.

Large-scale industry has yet to make much of a mark. Like most developing countries, Sri Lanka is anxious to expand its industry and has made great efforts to improve its basic services, especially in the provision of energy. One important project was to dam the Mahaweli river, in the north-east, to provide water and cheap electricity for that dry corner of the island. The authorities have also done their best to promote the country as a good place, with a cheap workforce, for Western companies to set up factories. They have had reasonable success – despite the political troubles – and local textile, shoe-making and electronics industries are all fairly prosperous. Fortunately, industrial expansion has not displaced the old craft skills embedded in Sri Lankan life: leather working, for example; producing finely engraved copper and bronzeware; and working the gemstones that are found in abundance in parts of the island.

Farming coconuts is another important business in Sri Lanka. An adult palm should yield up to 70 coconuts a year, and each part of the coconut can be put to a multitude of uses. Copra (the dried meat of the nut) is used, for example, in food products and cosmetics. Coir (fibre obtained from the husk) is used in making ropes, matting, brushes and brooms. The shell is burned as a fuel, while a form of alcoholic drink called arak *is distilled from the juice of the flower.*

Artists, dancers and cobra masks

In the arts, as in so many areas of Sri Lankan life, religion has always been an inspiration. Tucked away in many of the older temples are masterpieces of painting and sculpture, most of them little known. The area around Kandy has a wealth of temples, many hidden among rice paddies and jealously guarded by their Buddhist monks. One, at Lankatillke Viharaya, dating from the 13th century, sits dramatically on top of a rocky outcrop, overlooking a mingled landscape of rice paddies and forests. Its wooden façade is one seething mass of carving, as is the huge door opening into the temple. Inside, the floor is hewn from solid rock and carved into it, told in both the Tamil and the Sinhalese languages, is the story of the Sinhalese King Buwanekabahu who temporarily brought peace between the two races by marrying a Tamil princess.

Just outside Colombo, the temple of Kelaniya boasts a remarkable fresco cycle, painted only just over 50 years ago. It depicts episodes from the life of the Buddha and from the history of Buddhism in Sri Lanka: the story of the Indian princess who first brought the Buddha's tooth to the island, for example; and that of the Sinhalese princess, daughter of the Emperor Asoka, who brought a cutting from the sacred tree of Buddha to the royal court at Anuradhapura and planted it in a golden bowl. The frescoes have a vigour and originality that are worthy of the older Sri Lankan masters, as well as showing influences from outside, including the Italian primitives and modern naive painters.

Also largely inspired by religion are Sri Lanka's various forms of traditional dance, of which the most sophisticated and striking are the ritual dances from Kandy. The performers – who have been trained in the art from an early age – wear elaborate costumes, with ornately wrought silver headpieces, crossed belts covered with precious and semi-precious stones across their chests and heavy, decorative waist belts. The dances themselves were originally designed to celebrate and honour both the Buddha and the king – another reminder of how closely intertwined religion and political power were in the old kingdom of Kandy.

Another folk art consists of making strikingly carved and painted masks. It too has a religious inspiration – the masks are supposed to propitiate the various minor deities (some benevolent, others less so) who people the island's myths. They are made in small workshops, mostly in the south of the country, and there are three basic kinds: the *raksha*, used in religious dances and processions; the *kolam*, used in dramatic re-enactments of old legends; and the *sanni*, used chiefly in special dances that are believed to exorcise evil spirits. Some of these masks are particularly famous, notably the *naga raksha*, or cobra mask, inspired by the legend of the Rakshasas, a race of men who are said to have ruled Sri Lanka in ancient times. They had the alarming ability to turn themselves into cobras, thus terrifying their enemies, whom they made their slaves. Fortunately, the enslaved races called on the falcon-headed god Gurulu Raksha who came and killed the cobras. As a result, the head of a falcon is a recurring image in Sri Lankan art. Indeed, it might also be seen as a fitting image for Sri Lanka as a whole – for the island's age-old ability to survive the waves of conquerors that have swept over it and to remain true to its old self.

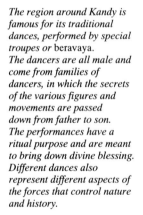

The region around Kandy is famous for its traditional dances, performed by special troupes or beravaya. *The dancers are all male and come from families of dancers, in which the secrets of the various figures and movements are passed down from father to son. The performances have a ritual purpose and are meant to bring down divine blessing. Different dances also represent different aspects of the forces that control nature and history.*

Maldives

One of the world's most exclusive tropical destinations has kept a firm check on the growth of tourism. Tourists there are, in growing numbers, but the people of the Maldives carry on fishing for shark and sailing from island to island in their traditional square-rigged boats. To this day, some have never seen a white person.

There are two reasons for this. In the first place, their isolated position in the Indian Ocean protects them from the worst excesses of mass tourism, even in the age of the jumbo jet. Secondly, successive governments of this fiercely Islamic republic have followed a strict policy of keeping islanders and tourists apart.

Coral Gems of the Indian Ocean

Previous page:
Bandos island is typical of the 2000 or so atolls – most of them uninhabited – that make up the Maldives: a coral reef covered with green vegetation.

Not all the islands are as tropically lush as this – many have no source of fresh water and so cannot support any inhabitants. On the 500-odd islands that are inhabited, most communities consist of small villages where fishermen and their families live in coral-built homes. Tourism is strictly confined to just 40 islands.

For centuries the Maldives have lived in near-isolation. A scattering of palm-fringed coral atolls spread out across the Indian Ocean south-west of Sri Lanka, they have gone their own way, largely untouched by the world's great events. The amount of ocean they cover is huge – 620 miles from north to south – but of the 2000 or so islands, just 500 are inhabited. Boats are still the only means of communication between the inhabited islands – and a leisurely one at that: it takes three or four days in a square-rigged *dhoni* to get from the north of the archipelago to the capital Malé in the centre. The only air links are between Malé and Colombo in Sri Lanka and Trivandrum in southern India.

The Maldives' loneliness is not wholly due to their geographical isolation. In 1965 they ceased to be a British protectorate and in 1968 a republic was proclaimed, bringing to an end more than 800 years of rule by sultans of the Didi dynasty. The new republican government was determined to preserve the country's special identity. It was (and remains) militantly Islamic – aligning itself with other Islamic countries such as Saudi Arabia – and is also committed to limiting the

spread of tourism, despite the islands' obvious appeal for visitors. A large and often oppressive bureaucracy means that any outsider wanting to set up a hotel or the like has to struggle through a thicket of regulations – which are constantly being changed.

One golden rule underlies this policy: no millionaire outsider is allowed to buy an entire island. Foreigners may lease islands from their Maldivian owners, but only for a certain period, which rarely exceeds ten years. Although these leases can theoretically be renewed, many are not. In some cases, the Maldivians will take islands back and run the facilities which foreign developers have set up. Visitors' visas and work permits are granted grudgingly, and are sometimes withdrawn without notice. To discourage people the government regards as 'drop-outs', it levies a tax of US$3 for every day a tourist spends on the islands. The result of all this is that only 40-odd islands have been developed for tourist use.

Another key principle is to try to make sure that tourists and locals are kept firmly apart. Tourist developments are allowed only on islands that were previously uninhabited; and there are no hotels on islands with a Maldivian population. The authorities cannot, of course, stop tourists from making day trips to islands where the local people live and from meeting some of them – but they make it as difficult as possible.

On the face of it, this severity towards tourists and tourism seems puzzling. After all, the Maldives form one of the poorest countries in the world, with an average yearly income of just US$180 per head, and the islands' chief economic hope undoubtedly lies in developing their tourist potential. They have no other natural resources – at present, three-quarters of the gross national product derives from fishing – and rely heavily on hand-outs from friendly Arab states and international organisations. An average life expectancy of 46 years – compared with 69 in Sri Lanka – shows how hard life

Few island women bother to wear veils, but in other respects the Maldivians are reasonably strict Muslims: alcohol is officially banned, for example. They are mostly descended from settlers from southern India or Sri Lanka who converted to Islam in the 12th century. Their language is Divehi, a form of Sinhalese.

The dhoni *is still the way most people get from island to island. It is wooden with one or two masts carrying a rectangular sail. Some families spend several months every year living on their* dhonis. *They trade in wood and coconuts between the capital, Malé, and the outermost islands, many of which lie several days' sailing time away.*

can be. And yet the government refuses to follow the example of other countries in a similar plight and with similar resources, because it is anxious to avoid the worse excesses of tourism. If there must be tourism, then it must come slowly and leave the islands' traditional ways of life as little touched as possible.

All of this has distinct advantages for the discerning visitor. During the 1980s some 40,000 tourists visited the Maldives most years – an average of only 1000 people on each of the 40 resort islands. It is all a far cry from the world of mass tourism. To make sure things stay this way, each of the resort islands has only enough rooms to accommodate between 40 and 100 people at any one time. Multi-storey buildings are forbidden – instead, hotels are attractively rambling bungalows built from coral stone with roofs of palm thatch. Needless to say, there is no such thing as pollution, and the sea life is among the richest in the world. The islands' capital, Malé, has just 20,000 inhabitants: the smell of drying fish lingers in streets drowsy with heat, there are few cars, and the easy going pace of life seems scarcely to have changed for centuries.

Visitors from the cold north step on to the tarmac at Hulule airport on Malé island – recently extended to take jumbo jets – to be greeted by a corrugated iron hut as arrival lounge and customs hall. Beyond lie rows of boats instead of the usual taxis or coaches. Colours are dazzlingly brilliant, and sea and sky seem to be unbelievably clear on the sea journey to one's chosen island. Once there, a range of possible activities lies open. Sporting enthusiasts can sample the marvels of the coral reefs with snorkel or, for the more daring, scuba diving outfit. There are also windsurfing, fishing (either deep-sea or in the lagoons that lie at the centre of many of the islands) and water skiing. Visitors of a less active bent doze the hours away on the beach or in the shade of coconut palms, or take boat trips to other islands, including those inhabited by the native Maldivians.

Faced with all this, it is easy for outsiders to think they have stumbled on an earthly paradise. Clearly, however, the Maldives are no paradise for those who live there, either the native Maldivians or the few foreign residents running the tourist industry. For the locals there is the constant battle against poverty; for the foreigners there is the aggravation of government interference in their business – though the government rarely pries into their financial dealings (there is even occasional talk in Malé of making the Maldives a tax haven). Few visitors, however, stay long enough to feel the weight of all these constraints. They return home with a lasting impression of waving palms, sparkling beaches and turquoise seas.

The Maldivians have always been great seafarers, who used to trade in tortoise shells, dried fish and ambergris with India. Most of them still spend large parts of their lives at sea – the boat is, after all, the most practical means of transport in the archipelago. The Maldivian dhoni *is particularly well suited to local conditions: flat-bottomed so that it can pass over most coral reefs, and with a huge sail to catch the smallest breath of wind.*

Malé is the capital and commercial centre of the Maldives. Boats from all the other islands converge on its harbour bringing their cargoes of fish, wood or coral. The town itself – founded by Portuguese traders in the 16th century – is suitably picturesque, with few motor vehicles and sandy streets that rapidly turn to mud when the frequent, short, sharp thunderstorms strike.

Pakistan

The state of Pakistan may be young, but it includes some of the oldest races on Earth. Founded in 1947 when British India was partitioned between Muslims and Hindus, Pakistan revolves in large measure around the Indus, the same river that gave birth to a series of flourishing civilisations from as early as 3000 BC. Today, the country has a special place as the meeting point of two very different worlds: Muslim Central Asia and the Indian subcontinent. Despite economic problems and a succession of political crises, it is trying to carve a new role for itself and to find a way of pulling all its divergent tribes and regions into a coherent whole.

Previous page:
Some of Pakistan's ethnic groups, such as the Sindhis, who include this old man, have histories dating back for thousands of years.

The Himalayan goat, or markhor (Capri falconeri), with its superbly spiralled horns, was still a fairly common sight in the mountains of Pakistan at the end of the 19th century. But a combination of local poachers and British game hunters depleted its numbers in the early years of this century. The species is now officially protected to save it from extinction.

Mist clings to the upper heights of the Swat Valley carving its way through the southern foothills of the Hindu Kush. Rocky mountain slopes like these dominate the landscape in northern Pakistan, punctuated at intervals by valleys such as Swat, Gilgit and Hunza. Despite the snows of winter and occasional summer storms, it is a dry region, rarely reached by the monsoon rains.

The Land of the Pure

A desert bordering on an inhospitable coast, where hot and humid winds blow across dunes and plains: Sind. A desert of dry mountains dotted here and there with pockets of fertility, baking hot in summer, icy cold in winter: Baluchistan, the haunt of smugglers plying their illegal trade with neighbouring Iran. Plains and a fertile plateau irrigated by streams and rivers: the Punjab. Mountains broken up into majestic ranges and home to fierce warrior tribes: the legendary North-West Frontier Province. Perched on the edge of the Himalayas, among glacier-covered peaks: Baltistan and the valley of Gilgit, both part of Kashmir. One of the world's great rivers descending its monumental stairway from the heights of Tibet to the Arabian Sea: the Indus. All these and more comprise the landscape of Pakistan.

The country that came into being when the Indian subcontinent was partitioned between Muslims and Hindus in 1947 undoubtedly offers some of the most stunning scenery on Earth. At the same time, it presents a number of anomalies. Politically, it can hardly call itself a unified country at all. It is more a collection of nations, where local and tribal loyalties are strong – a legacy, in part, of British rule (lasting until 1947) which encouraged such loyalties. Admittedly, Pakistan makes more sense as a unified whole since Bangladesh (the former East Pakistan) went its own way after a brief war – in which India became involved on the side of the Bangladeshis – in 1971. Even so, successive governments have had to steer a course through a mix of centralism, federalism, tribalism and local autonomies. Pakistan's position close to the troubled regions of Afghanistan and the Middle East has lent it strategic importance, hence the support, by and large, of Western governments, despite regular periods of military dictatorship. But no amount of outside backing has affected the diversity of its society – which also provides Pakistan's colour and appeal for the visitor.

Western backing has proved useful for ambitious engineering projects, such as the harnessing of the hydroelectric and irrigation potential of the Indus and the building of the Karakorum Highway deep into the mountains of the north. In undertaking such projects, the authorities have hoped not only to foster economic growth but also to tame the wilder parts of their country. Slowly but surely, they hope to bring the multiplicity of languages and dialects, of local customs and usages more fully into the orbit of the centralised state. It is an uphill task, especially among the tiny ethnic communities of the remoter mountain areas and the larger tribal federations of the north-west. It is also a policy that will destroy some of the colour of Pakistan's local traditions and ways of life.

The pieces of the mosaic

Low rainfall and high levels of evaporation when the rains do come mean that Pakistan relies almost entirely for water on the snows of the mountains when they melt in spring and early summer and, even more, on the Indus and its tributaries. In many ways, indeed, the Indus is to the 110.4 million Pakistanis what the Nile is to the Egyptians – and it occupies a roughly equivalent place in the imagination of the people. Its 1700-mile journey from the Himalayas to the sea is certainly awe-inspiring. Swift-running and turbulent in its upper reaches, it emerges into Pakistani Kashmir south of the Karakorum Range before skirting the northern slopes of Nanga Parbat (at 26,660 feet, one of the world's highest peaks). It then threads a passage through dramatic gorges, some of them 10,000 feet deep, before reaching the plateau of Potwar, near the capital Islamabad. Here, at last, the river's pace slackens, allowing it to deposit millions of tons of fertile silt each year on the plains of the south.

Rough roads, good enough for four-wheel-drive vehicles, have recently been built in the remote regions around Chitral in the north. The authorities hope that this will help to modernise the area, mostly inhabited by Kalash tribespeople. Equally, though, it exposes the local, non-Muslim culture to the twin threats of tourism and absorption into the Islamic mainstream.

Even in the south it remains a capricious and sometimes dangerous presence which has changed its course several times. Standing as witnesses to this are fortresses and small towns that once guarded fording points but now lie isolated in the vast plain, often abandoned by all but the sand and a few crows. Every change of course had drastic effects on the local economy: networks of irrigation channels became redundant, and new ones had to be built. Nowadays, this danger has largely been removed by the construction of dams – including some of the largest and most elaborate in the world – along both the Indus itself and its Punjabi tributaries such as the Sutlej, Ravi, Chenab and Jhelum.

The taming of the Indus has made possible the greater development of the south's agriculture and industry. At the same time, the building of the Karakorum Highway has had important effects on the high valleys of the far north. Building at all was a gamble, depending not just on the skills of the engineers but also on cooperation with the Communist Chinese authorities – it links Islamabad with the Chinese frontier at the 15,100-foot Khunjerab Pass. In so far as the road was intended to pull together the northern areas of Pakistan, the gamble

Kalash children play in the fields near their village. Agriculture dominates the lives of the Kalash – their community life as well as their religion and festivals. Their main crops are wheat in spring and maize in summer. Tasks are allocated according to sex. Women work in the fields, but the men look after the livestock, since this involves long periods away from home when the flocks are grazing their mountain pastures.

has paid off. To reach Gilgit from the capital used to mean several days' hard driving; it now takes ten hours. This has military significance: troops can easily be rushed to regions of Kashmir disputed between Pakistan and India. The highway has also opened up the north for tourism (a growing money-spinner in Pakistan), and locally grown agricultural produce can be exported more easily. Inevitably, it has led to some dilution of local cultures.

One of these, which survives with many of its old ways intact, is centred on Skardu at the heart of the wild mountain region of Baltistan. The Balti people are Muslim by faith but Tibetan by race, and a mingling of Tibetan and Muslim influences is noticeable in their communities. Houses of stone and wood rise several

storeys high as in Tibet, while inside they are warrens of narrow corridors and dark stairways. The stepped roofs of the older mosques are more reminiscent of the Buddhist pagodas of Tibet than the domes of traditional mosques – though the newer structures are more obviously Islamic.

Despite the arrival of the Karakorum Highway, life is hard in this bleak region. Outside the towns and villages, fields are rocky, sloping plots of ground that have been carved out only by centuries of painful labour. Again the Tibetan influence is clearly present: in the use of the dzo (a cross between a bull and a female yak) as the principal beast of burden, and in a taste for hot rancid butter, particularly in winter. In summer, fruit adds variety to the diet, above all the apricots for which northern Pakistan is famous.

The last 'infidels'

Another of Pakistan's minority peoples are the 2500-strong Kalash, living in the valleys of the Brir, Bumberet and Rumbur rivers near Chitral in the north-west. They were believed to be descendants of mercenaries who fought for Alexander the Great and settled here after his invasion of India in 327 BC. This theory is still popular with many people, though the Kalash themselves have never held it.

Whatever their origins, the Kalash (or Kafir Kalash, 'Black Infidels') are a unique people. Above all, unlike almost all other Pakistanis, they are non-Muslims, though social pressures mean that Islam has been making inroads among them, despite government assurances that the rights of minority races, including their religious rights, will be respected. Some of the strongest pressure comes from their closest neighbours, the Khos or Chitralis. The rivalry between these two peoples goes back centuries to when the Kalash were dominant. Since then the Kalash have been pushed back ever farther into their mountain valleys. The opening of rough roads good enough for four-wheel-drive vehicles and the growth of tourism in the valleys have recently brought in extra income, at the cost of endangering an irreplaceable culture. Knowing how to balance the benefits of modernisation with the integrity of ancient ways is a constant puzzle for the authorities in the north and west of Pakistan.

The Kalash way of life, like that of the Baltis, has been hard. Unlike the Baltis, they have never used beasts of burden, relying on their own arms and legs to exploit scanty pieces of cultivable land. Their colourful customs have earned them popularity among the tourists. Particularly striking are the headdresses – *kupas* – of the women. These are elaborate structures based on a band of thick black cloth, some six to eight inches wide, wrapped around the head with a tail hanging down behind as far as the small of the back. Sewn on to this are festoons of small bells, metal trinkets and cowrie shells (tiny white shells, shaped rather like coffee beans, which for the Kalash symbolise femininity). Generally speaking, the full regalia of the *kupas* is kept for special occasions. For everyday use, adult women – and young girls not yet old enough to

Of all the Hindu Kush's various kafir ('infidel' – that is, non-Muslim) tribes, the Kalash are the only one whose women wear the kupas. This is the elaborate headdress decked out with a large pompom on top and an assortment of buttons, metal trinkets and, above all, cowrie shells. The shells, which reach the area from the Maldives and Philippines by way of Afghanistan, are much valued. For centuries they were used as a form of currency. To the Kalash they symbolise fertility.

The staples of the Kalash diet are unleavened bread and milk. The bread is made on hot metal plates known as hunza and preparing it is normally a a task for the women. Kalash kitchens are dark and smoky, since they have no proper vents or windows.

have a *kupas* – wear a smaller *shushut*. This is a band of red, black or multi-coloured cloth, about two inches wide, wrapped this time around the back of the head, again with a tail hanging down behind. The decorations are less elaborate than for the *kupas* but are striking enough, often including a few cowrie shells or white shirt buttons and coral and turquoise gems. The coral theme is picked up in the necklaces which Kalash women wear in imposing arrays – some wearing as many as 20 or more.

In contrast, Kalash women's dresses are simple affairs made from plain black or dark brown cloth hanging down straight without any styling or ornament. The cloth needs to be hard-wearing, for most women own just two dresses in their adult lifetime, sometimes wearing one on top of the other. When a woman dies, one of the dresses is buried with her, while the other is inherited by her eldest daughter. Dresses are supposed to pass down for several generations; in practice, it seems there is some flexibility. One dress is not likely to last more than two generations.

Kalash men have long since abandoned their traditional flowing robes and adopted the more practical costume of the Khos, which is more or less identical to that worn by men throughout Pakistan. This is the *shalwar-kameez*, a combination of baggy trousers and long shirt. On their heads many Kalash men still wear the *kashunk*, a woollen beret which is common to many of the local peoples.

The Kalash religion is distinctive. Like the Muslims, they believe in one god, whom they call Roudai. Since he may not be approached directly, they have to rely on four intercessors, who are immortal and venerated but not divine; they may be relics of ancestor-worship. The Kalash religion is fast dying out as anything other than a ceremonial affair whose chief importance is as an expression of Kalash patriotism. It also provides a good excuse for festivals, local traditions of music and dancing.

In the beginning was poetry

These regional traditions abound in Pakistan. But there are also more nationwide traditions associated with songs composed in the Urdu language. Urdu – the one tongue, apart from English, which is spoken to some

Strict Muslims wash themselves ritually before each of the five daily prayer sessions – in order to cleanse their bodies in the same way that they are cleansing their spirits through prayer. At the centre of its courtyard every mosque has a fountain or water basin which is used for this purpose.

The great Badshahi Mosque in Lahore was built in 1674 during the reign of the Mogul Emperor Aurangzeb. It can hold 60,000 people at prayer and was for a long time the largest mosque in Asia – only in 1987 was it overtaken by the new Faisal Mosque in Islamabad.

degree throughout Pakistan – was born in the Middle Ages as a kind of *lingua franca* used by the armed followers of the Mogul emperors. It originally consisted of a mix of Hindi, Arabic and Persian, with a few Turkish terms thrown in as well, but rapidly became an important language in its own right, thriving alongside local tongues such as Punjabi, Sindhi and Baluchi. Under the British Raj it came to be seen above all as the language of the subcontinent's Muslims and, as a result, was chosen as Pakistan's national language at the time of independence – even though many of the new nation's leaders, including Mohammed Ali Jinnah, the *Qa'id-e A'zam* or Great Leader, spoke little Urdu and were more at ease with English.

Over the centuries, Urdu came to be used as often as the local languages when composing poetry. The traditions of Urdu poetry that continue to flourish include songs (*geets*) and poems of love (*ghazals*), besides religious poems, often with a strong mystical element. Among the best known of the religious forms are the *qawwali*, long chants recited to hypnotic rhythms beaten out on a pair of small hand drums or *tablas*. The cinema and television may have made inroads on popular culture, but the Pakistanis still relish these poetic traditions. One of their nation's spiritual fathers, the philosopher and anti-British political leader Mohammed Iqbal – whose works were a key influence in the revival of Islamic culture throughout the East in

The most important prayer session each week is at midday on Friday. In some places – like here in Quetta – the mosques are too small to hold all the worshippers, so they have to spill out on to the streets.

The gleaming domes of the Mahabat Khan or White Mosque rise above the alleys of Peshawar's bazaar. Lying so close to the Afghan frontier and the Khyber Pass, Peshawar was for centuries a crossroads on the caravan routes linking central Asia and the Indian subcontinent. More recently, business people have benefited from the influx of refugees escaping the fighting across the border in Afghanistan.

Posters publicise films showing at the local cinema. The Pakistanis, like the Indians, are keen cinemagoers and have their own flourishing film industry – more notable on the whole for the quantity than the quality of its products. Efforts have been made in the past to raise the films' artistic standards, but local tastes are firmly in favour of straightforward heroes and stars, rather than obscure messages and subtle artistry.

attractive cities. For many people it is as lacking in character now as when it was inaugurated as capital in 1967.

Lahore, by contrast, is a place of exuberant bustle and life, a mass of seeming contradictions that give it much of its appeal. Among the more confusing aspects of Lahori life is the extent of Western influence. A city which boasts more publishing houses than any other in the country can easily absorb and adapt foreign attitudes and customs. Civil servants, businessmen, engineers and the like often wear Western-style suits to work, but at the weekends change into the traditional *shalwar-kameez* for picnics in one of the numerous parks. Instead of veils, some women wrap silk scarves around their faces which match their brightly coloured long tunics and baggy trousers. A woman can use a corner of the scarf to veil part of her face in a supremely coquettish gesture. Among children things are equally confused. Some wear traditional dress; for others T-shirt and jeans is the standard everyday wear.

City bazaars and the tribal heritage

Friday – the weekly day of rest – may see the citizens of Lahore relaxing and picnicking in their parks, but for the remainder of the week the city, and above all its bazaars, swarms with people and noisy activity. In the bazaar, the points where alleys meet and cross are congested with pedestrians, motorcycles and *tongas* (two-wheeled, horse-drawn carts). There is rarely any shortage of goods. Stallholders spill their wares on to

The camel, a pack animal in most of central and southern Asia, is also used to pull carts in Pakistan. Though these have been supplanted by motor vehicles on the highways, they are still common in the bazaars. In the mountains of Baluchistan and the North-West Frontier, meanwhile, camels are prized for their wool, milk and meat.

the early 20th century – was also a poet of considerable distinction. Nowadays, Pakistanis of all races and levels of education, from Baluchi tribesmen gathered round their fires at night to intellectuals gathered in the salons of Lahore, compose and recite poetry for entertainment. The modernisation of their society has not diminished this basic love of rhythm and the power of the word.

The centre of modern Pakistani culture is undoubtedly Lahore, today capital of the Punjab and in the time of the great Emperor Akbar (1556-1605) one of the principal cities of the Mogul Empire. In the 1950s, the authorities decided to transfer the national capital from Karachi, with its overcrowded shanty towns and constant risk of epidemics. Lahore seemed a perfect alternative. In the end, it was passed over, in part because it was less than 20 miles from the Indian frontier. Relations between the two countries were tense then as they often have been since, and a spot less open to invasion was finally selected. Islamabad, built from scratch during the early 1960s, also had the advantage that it was close to Rawalpindi, the general headquarters of Pakistan's army. It is not one of the country's most

the pavements, where they compete for space with itinerant sellers. Each alley has its own speciality, and assails the senses with a characteristic combination of smells and colours.

The most colourful stalls are those which sell 'garlands of notes'. These are given as presents on occasions such as weddings, and are believed to bring good luck and prosperity. They are made from two strips of paper or cloth, about two inches wide, which are first decorated with gold sequins, tiny crepe bows and small red or blue balls of wool or cotton. The two strips are then joined at the top with a piece of string –

sometimes also decorated with wool or cotton balls – which will be used to hang the garland around the neck of the person to whom it is given. At the bottom hangs a large, gaudy heart made from tinsel. The edges of the garland, meanwhile, are adorned with its strangest feature: rows and rows of banknotes. Usually, these are one-rupee notes, but higher denominations are sometimes used.

The pace of life in Peshawar – less than 30 miles east of the Khyber Pass on the Afghan frontier – is more deliberate. These two cities boast Pakistan's most famous bazaars but the atmosphere in each is different. Lahore's bazaar has all the diversity and exuberance of the Indian subcontinent; Peshawar's reflects the more austere air of central Asia. Although Peshawar has been inundated since 1979 with Afghan refugees fleeing the fighting in their native land, they have not transformed the feel of the place. Most of the refugees are tribespeople, largely indistinguishable in customs and language from their Pathan kinsmen living in and around Peshawar.

Peshawar is a frontier city in two senses. It is the most important Pakistani city on the border with Afghanistan, but it also lies on the boundary of the Pathan tribal areas. These are zones with a high degree of local autonomy, where, according to the Pakistani constitution, the writ of the central or provincial authorities applies only if it has been ratified by the *jirga*, the deliberative council of the tribal chiefs. This means that national legislation is almost invariably modified to make it fit in with local traditions. Only in cases of the utmost national importance are the central authorities allowed to override the tribal chiefs.

The Pathans are not Pakistan's only tribespeople. To

A stallholder whisks the flies off his produce in a bazaar on the North-West Frontier. In these mountain regions few men go anywhere without their rifles – most of them made by local gunsmiths.

A herd of buffalo is driven through the narrow lanes of Lahore's main bazaar, adding to the congestion. The Lahore bazaar, along with Peshawar's, is among the largest in the world – a labyrinth of alleys where buyers and sellers jostle for space among the confusion. Changes may be affecting some parts of Pakistani life, but the bazaar continues to thrive in a society where the supermarket and shopping mall have yet to make their mark.

Trucks and motor cars are more than simply a means of transport . . . they are also works of art. The vehicle may be ancient but the owner will lavish care upon it and often, as here, ornament it in extravagant fashion.

the south and west, the tribes of Baluchistan present a pattern of some complexity, where the dominant Baluchi – themselves descended from a variety of different peoples – live alongside smaller groups such as the Brahui.

The Brahui are particularly intriguing. They are descended from the Dravidians – the original inhabitants of large parts of the subcontinent – and may well be the last survivors of the races that created a remarkable civilisation on the banks of the Indus in the middle of the 3rd millennium BC. Pushed back by later invaders into the bleak regions of Makran, in the south of modern Baluchistan, the Brahui came into contact with the Baluchi when they arrived from southern central Asia several centuries later. Although heavily outnumbered by the newcomers, the Brahui somehow managed to survive as a distinct group. They formed tribal alliances with the Baluchi against common enemies, but at the same time hung on to their old language and many of their old ways. Today, the two groups are still allied, though subject to periodic bouts of internal rivalry.

The lost tribes of Baluchistan

In spite of recent discoveries of oil and gas in Baluchistan, the province remains backward, with the lowest literacy rate in Pakistan – 5 per cent. It is also among the most traditional. The Baluchi rely on the ways of their ancestors to eke out their livings. Some are peasant farmers – not an easy occupation in a region where, with the exception of the area around the provincial capital, Quetta, rainfall is scarce and rivers few. Some traditionally resort to smuggling, though this trade is in decline since the authorities have started patrolling the border with Iran more thoroughly. Others are nomads, tending flocks of sheep and goats. Camels used to be their means of transport in this near-desert landscape, but these have declined with the arrival of motor vehicles.

Animals have a precise significance in the nomadic way of life. As one Baluchi saying puts it: 'If you see a cow, the well is not far off; if you see a donkey, you are within sight of a camp; if you see a camel, you are lost.' Each has its place as a provider of food. Cows' milk, goats' milk, ewes' milk and camels' milk are all staples of the local diet, while mutton is the nomads' favourite meat. Long evenings spent under cover of black tents made from woven goats' hair are when they enjoy *sajji*, a leg of mutton roasted on a vertical spit. This is rotated inside an oven made from stones which have been heated in a fire. Preparing the oven is generally the task

Pakistani bazaars sell a huge variety of goods. The most colourful part of the bazaar sells everything needed for weddings. Stalls and shops compete to provide all the luxury and colour any married couple could desire: rolls of rich silks, gold and jewellery, and the extraordinary garlands of notes (ornamented, as their name suggests, with banknotes) that are supposed to bring good luck. Here, in the bazaar at Peshawar, banks of flowers add another colourful element.

Bands of musicians still wander around Pakistan, providing the entertainment for both religious and secular celebrations. Although music and poetry are part of normal life for most Pakistanis, the musicians themselves are not highly regarded. After centuries in which Islam has been the region's dominant religion, they still suffer from vestiges of Hindu caste prejudice.

of the men, while the women look after the cooking. Also characteristic of the Baluchi diet is the use of herbs and plants that the herdsmen gather as they move their flocks between summer and winter pastures; some of the most distinctive come from the mountain pastures where they retreat in the heat of summer.

The dwarf palms that grow along the edges of the oases have their place, too. Palm hearts are a popular delicacy among the Baluchi, while their leaves provide the strong fibres used to make a variety of practical items, from matting to sandals, primitive spoons to the tubes of hookah pipes. The leaves are also sometimes used to construct small, makeshift tents and in summer people make them into fans.

Usually the women are in charge of these crafts, as well as of the more sophisticated art of weaving carpets,

Until recently, it seemed as if many of Pakistan's craft traditions were dying out. In the last few years, cities such as Hyderabad in Sind have set up workshops to encourage craftsmen to carry on with their trades. In this way, people hope to keep alive age-old skills, such as making the rich jewellery that for centuries has been the pride of nomads and countrywomen.

The suroze *is the favourite instrument of the wandering musicians of Baluchistan and Sind. They play it, as here, tucked between their legs, drawing a bow across the strings like a violin. A traditional musician like this one will spend his life moving from village to village, nomadic encampment to encampment, playing for people in the evenings and receiving food and clothing in return.*

and they are trained from a very early age. Carpets are among the chief ornaments in most Baluchis' tents and homes; they also provide a useful supplement to their incomes, since they fetch high prices in the bazaars. The Baluchis themselves rarely go into the larger cities to sell their wares (in any case, the province has only two cities of any size, Quetta and Kalat) and as non-Baluchi merchants are reluctant to venture into a region known for its wildness, the smaller, local merchants serve as middlemen.

The communities living around Baluchistan's fringes have always led a different life to that of their kinsmen in the interior. In many cases they have been more prosperous. Towns such as Turbat and Panjgaur, for example, have long flourished on cross-border trade, both legal and illegal, with Iran. In recent years, turbulence in Iran and Afghanistan, and the tighter control the central authorities have imposed on the area as a result, have damped down the local economy. The border regions have also suffered from their isolation: roads are mostly primitive and sometimes dangerous –

and out of bounds to foreigners without a special permit.

More open to the outside world are the coastal towns of Makran, of which Gwadar was once staging post for Arab merchant fleets returning from the Far East. Nowadays, these towns are homes to fishermen who make their living from the rich waters of the Arabian Sea. There are similar communities farther east along the coast of Sind as well as in the marshy areas fringing the mouth of the Indus. Curiously, although these fishing communities bring a welcome variety to the Pakistani diet, their people are often treated with contempt by their countrymen – an example of caste prejudice that has survived from pre-Islamic times.

A Baluchi tribesman is splendidly wrapped up against the desert sands and heat. Many Baluchis still live as nomads, travelling the deserts with their flocks of goats, sheep, a few cattle and above all camels. To survive the rigours of the climate, especially the high winds which in summer blow for weeks on end, they have evolved elaborate costumes consisting of several protective layers of woollen and cotton garments.

Pakistan's fishermen have, however, seen some improvements in recent years. Well-equipped fishing ports have been built at Karachi and Gwadar. Here, the several hundred vessels crammed in alongside each other are often both home and workplace for their crews, especially the younger ones and those whose families live far away. Elsewhere, conditions tend to be more primitive, particularly among the river and lake fishing communities where people often use the same methods their ancestors employed for centuries.

These inland fishing communities are often places of considerable charm. Small villages with tall houses built from baked clay line the banks of the lake or river, mingling farming with fishing to earn their livelihood.

The sun governs the day's activities. Men and women get up the moment the sky begins to lighten in order to catch the coolest part of the day. Everyone sets about his or her special tasks: letting the farm animals out of their barns, heading for the fields or fishing boats, fetching water from the well or stream. By the time the sun has reached its zenith around midday, the greater part of the day's jobs will have been done and, during summer, village and countryside sink into somnolence as people shelter from the heat. In winter, the pattern is slightly different: the nights are cold and the sun only begins to warm the air around mid-morning. As a result, the heat is bearable even at midday and people are able to go on working in the fields.

Gathering thorn bushes is a time-honoured ritual among the Baluchis, both the nomads and the settled farmers. Cakes of dried dung provide their basic fuel, but they also need the twigs of thorn to help to get their fires going. Unfortunately, this has led to severe problems of deforestation. The authorities are now encouraging the planting of trees, as well as alternative energy sources such as solar power, but such programmes are slow to take effect.

Tradition and freedom

In the late afternoon a gentle breeze starts to blow and the peasant women who were working unveiled during the morning cover their faces once more. Working in the fields is one of the few occasions when it is regarded as seemly for women to go out in public unveiled. For the rest of the time when they go out, they always have their faces covered. For food, most families are more or less self-sufficient, growing the crops they need on their plots of land and raising a few head of livestock – thus there is little need for women to go to any shops. Selling surplus produce is a male affair. In times of natural disaster, the government offers financial aid to the peasants – but again the process of collecting the aid and exchanging it for much-needed goods is handled by the men.

If a woman does leave her home alone, it is probably to pay her respects at one of the small shrines which are scattered throughout Pakistan, most of them the tombs of some local holy man. Once there, the woman will spend some time in meditation and prayer, perhaps asking for the healing of an illness or for a baby boy – most families still set special store by male children. The larger shrines often have a small stall where pilgrims can buy garlands of flowers to lay on the tomb as offerings, glass bracelets (also traditionally used as offerings) and a few religious books, including, of course, the works, if any, of the person buried there. In some areas, the woman's priority on entering the shrine will almost certainly be to buy a few glass bracelets. She will then head for the tomb and ritually smash them on it; this is seen as a sign of devotion. Having offered up her prayers, the woman buys some more glass bracelets and then goes home.

Back in the village, other scenes are unfolding. In the nearest pond or river, children splash happily around good-natured buffaloes. According to official statistics two children in three go to school, but in reality many go only when they have nothing else to do. In the heat of summer in the southern parts of the country, most prefer to wallow in the coolness of the streams – unless, of course, the school itself provides some refuge from the heat. In the mountains of the north, the cold and deep snows of winter keep children out of school. And yet the authorities go on building schools in the hope of rapidly defeating illiteracy. In the tribal areas every aspect of educational policy has to be agreed by the chiefs; and in the country as a whole, parents who are themselves illiterate have to be convinced of the importance of education for their children.

Although attitudes are changing, there is still a great deal of suspicion about education. The state-run school is seen by many country people as an instrument of the mistrusted central authorities. Private establishments have higher standards than the state schools and are more generally appreciated. But they are also beyond the pockets of all but the well-to-do. One alternative is the *madrasa*, or Koranic school; once the child has learnt how to read the Koran and been taught the key religious principles, however, he will consider his education there finished. These problems are less acute for those living in towns and cities where parents have the choice of the best schools, both state-run and private.

The authorities have tried to spread around these relative benefits enjoyed by the cities. At the start of their careers, teachers – and doctors – are encouraged to spend two years working in a village. These can often be tough years for young people emerging from further education and cast adrift in an environment they have never experienced before or have long since left behind.

The disparity between the numbers of primary and secondary schools in Pakistan speaks loudly of another problem with education. In 1983–84 – in a country where over half the population was under 15 years old – there were 55,000 primary schools, and just 8000

Terraces of greenery climb the awesome, rocky slopes of the Hunza Valley, where it carves its way through the southern outcrops of the Pamir mountains. In the foreground, a woman picks through a harvest of apricots. Hunza is known for the exceptional succulence of its fruit.

Apricots are the chief delicacy of northern Pakistan, growing prolifically throughout the valleys of the north. People eat them fresh in season – August onwards – and dried during the winter months, when they are the chief source of sugar in the local diet.

The people of Hunza – or Hunzakuts – are famed for their longevity, which they put down to the tonic effects of eating so many apricots. They lived in isolation from the rest of the world until the Karakorum Highway reached their region.

Balti women and children work in the fields at Satapara, near Skardu. As well as producing fruit and some cereals, the more sheltered valleys in the north also grow a few root crops, such as potatoes and turnips.

secondary schools. A mere 2 per cent of the population goes on to university. The problem of producing a well-educated local workforce is compounded, in Pakistan as in many developing countries, by the brain drain of those who have reached the highest levels of education taking up more lucrative jobs in Europe or North America.

Disparities between the sexes in a male-dominated society provide another often contentious issue. In education, these grow fewer the higher you get: at the secondary school level, boy pupils far outnumber girls, but at the universities the difference is much smaller. The reason for this is that university students tend to come from the more privileged, and hence Westernised, sectors of the population. In these a girl's education is usually considered as important as a boy's – even if girls, once married, are more likely than not to end up as housewives. Disparities are more clearly pronounced in the job market. A number of junior administrative posts

For centuries, the Brahui have lived in close alliance with their more powerful neighbours, the Baluchis. They are, however, the older race, descended from the original Dravidian inhabitants of the Indus Valley. This Brahui woman is working on a piece of the embroidery for which Brahuis, Baluchis and Pathans are all famous. Among most of Pakistan's tribal people, the more richly embroidered your costume, the higher your social status.

are occupied by women, but few reach the highest levels. Only a handful of professions such as medicine and nursing, teaching and the law offer real openings. Pakistan is still a state where 90 per cent of women are illiterate and only 2 per cent do paid work.

For most women, marriage and child-bearing are the destinies they have to look forward to – and in most cases happily accept. Marriage comes early by Western standards: between the ages of 13 and 19. It will be arranged by the two families – the girl and boy concerned are rarely consulted – and the ceremonies celebrating it will be sumptuous and costly. After that, the young bride's life will be very much dominated by her mother-in-law – until her own children grow up and she in turn can domineer over a brood of daughters-in-

law. This, of course, assumes that she has at least some male children. If fortune fails to favour the family and the first two children are girls, there is little chance of the mother and father respecting the advice of the family planning services: these try to encourage people to have no more than two children. Only among the urban upper middle classes do such recommendations carry much weight.

Economic factors have long limited the number of men taking more than one wife – though polygamy still arouses fierce arguments between modernists (who are against it) and traditionalists (who are in favour). As for women's groups, their demands are modest. They tend to appeal simply to Koranic principles, which would limit the worst social abuses, most of them the legacy of local traditions. Not that all these traditions keep the woman rigidly veiled and in the home. In the valleys of the north, for example, in Baltistan and among the non-Muslim Kalashs, women go everywhere unveiled. In these societies they enjoy comparative freedom – it can come as something of a surprise to visitors from the south when a woman returning from the fields accosts them on a mountain path and engages in casual conversation.

Looking to the future

Pakistan has been both the victim and the beneficiary of the circumstances that brought it into being. Certainly, the first few decades of its existence have been far from trouble-free. The country has been torn between Western-style modernism and growing Islamic fundamentalism. It suffers from a gruelling climate which can make the simplest forms of agriculture an uphill task, and on the diplomatic front has endured fraught relations with its neighbours on all sides. And yet, in spite of these problems, Pakistani society has never grown stagnant. Its culture remains vibrant. Its economy manages to survive. Its cities and towns frequently surprise by their cleanliness and air of prosperity.

It all represents a considerable achievement, made the more remarkable by the stresses imposed during the 1980s when more than 3 million Afghan refugees flooded into the country. Various factors helped to alleviate these strains and to avoid damaging conflicts: government and international aid, as well as the ties of kinship that bound many of the refugees to the locals. Even so, this extra burden was a threat to a fragile equilibrium, both environmental and economic. It also highlighted some of Pakistan's own difficulties. Indeed, many Pakistanis welcomed the arrival of the refugees as a means of brushing up their country's image; this had been tarnished by the execution in 1979 of Zulfikar Ali Bhutto, the prime minister thrown out of office after the military coup in July 1977. But, if the refugees did help in this respect, they also emphasised other areas of tension: the huge gap between the Westernised upper classes of the cities and the rugged traditionalism of most of the rest of the population. The Soviet withdrawal from Afghanistan in February 1989 did little to ease the problem. Fighting continued between the different Afghan factions and it was a long time before many refugees felt safe enough to return to their homeland.

Problems there have been, and many of them remain. But still Pakistani life goes on. On the patch of open ground at the edge of a village, two teams of riders face each other in an informal game of polo. An ancient but lovingly painted truck clatters through the village, honking its horn. In tribal areas, village men, rifles and ammunition belts slung over their shoulders, make their way out to the fields. A buffalo treads round and round, turning a squealing millstone which grinds the flour for *nan* and *chapattis* (thin unleavened bread). In the plains spreading out from the Indus, a man dozes the hot afternoon away at home, occasionally stirring the air by tugging on a small shutter which opens on to a special air vent leading up to the roof. In Karachi, a businessman or civil servant works on, sweltering in a

A village baker makes piles of the chapattis – *thin unleavened bread – that are among the staples of the Pakistani diet. He first forms the dough into small cakes, then plasters the cakes against the walls of an underground brick oven. After a while, he opens the oven and removes the cooked* chapattis *with metal skewers.*

The wilderness regions of Baluchistan can be as cold in winter as they are baking hot in summer. To protect themselves from the cold – as well as the summer dust – the nomads cover the floors of their tents with rugs. Here, a rug is being woven on one of the rudimentary horizontal looms that are still common among the nomads. The advantage of these – unlike the more sophisticated affairs used nowadays by the non-nomads – is that they are so easy to dismantle and then put up again on another site.

smart bush-shirt or *kurta* with an air-conditioning unit standing idle beside him thanks to a power cut.

As Pakistan enters the 21st century it will be facing all the dilemmas of a poor country heavily reliant on donations of foreign aid from the U.S. and rich Arab neighbours. And, despite being self-sufficient in products like steel and cotton (two of its chief exports) it is obliged to import essential commodities such as petroleum and chemicals. In common with other multi-ethnic, schismatic countries, Pakistan has had to weather intense internal struggles. In two decades of turbulent political upheaval, the country has seen 10 years of the strictly conservative and militaristic rule of President Zia and the subsequent, sensational election of the charismatic prime minister, Benazir Bhutto. Under the leadership of the current premier, Mohammad Nawaz Sharif, elected with a large majority in 1990, the country has entered a period of relative stability.

The major problem facing the present government is one of expansion. Over the next thirty years, the current population figure of around 105 million will have increased to more than 200 million. Two-thirds of the country's inhabitants are concentrated in the rural areas, where customs and living conditions remain firmly in the past. An erratic climate, subject to devastating earthquakes and heavy seasonal flooding has done little to help the beleaguered agricultural communities still employing antiquated farming methods and fiercely resistant to change. Nevertheless, crops have benefited greatly from the recent introduction of farming schemes able to counter the effects of salinity and waterlogging. These innovations are invaluable to an industry which employs over half of the working population.

Conquering the huge illiteracy rate is more difficult. The vast difference between the sophistication of Lahore - Pakistan's intellectual "core" - for instance, and the remote bleakness of Baltistan, where education is practically non-existent, is a vivid example of the country's paradoxical nature. In a country three times the size of the United Kingdom, there are less than 30 universities and only 2 per cent of young people attend higher education. Feudal law continues to survive in the tribal areas, and democracy has often been the victim of a society which has yet to endorse a common national identity.

To the Western visitor, Pakistan is endlessly inviting. From the days when intrepid Himalayan expeditions attempted to scale the glacial heights of K2, it has become an essential port of call for a constant stream of travellers - the 'back-packers' following the Central Asian trail, en route to or from India, China and Tibet. Pakistan is aware that it must encourage its tourist trade, which brings in a much needed income. For the government, the key to success will be found in striking the right balance between retaining the traditional elements, the cultural attractions which have their roots in the ancient civilisations of the Indus Valley and the Mughal race while incorporating all the benefits of a modern programme for survival.

Pakistan is emerging as one of the most vibrant third world countries in the Commonwealth and is facing the future with the energy and enthusiasm of a young nation determined to capitalise on its considerable natural resources and sustain a burgeoning economy.

Two small boys play on the back of a good-natured buffalo. This is the height of summer when children and buffaloes alike take refuge from the midday heat in waterways flooded by the monsoon rains. Unlike their neighbours in India, the Pakistanis do not regard the buffalo as in any way sacred. It is an important animal, none the less: their chief beast of burden, as well as provider of milk (often made into the delicious local yoghurt), meat and leather.

Burma

Despite its wealth of natural resources, Burma, or Myanmar as it is officially named, is one of the ten poorest nations in the world. This is largely a result of the Burmese government's isolationist policies. But these policies have made Burma one of the most unspoilt countries in Asia. Dense forest, dominated by teak and rubber trees, covers two thirds of the country. The Irrawaddy, Burma's great, meandering river, flows down its centre, from the northern hills, past acres of rice fields around Mandalay to the south and Rangoon. Here, the bustling capital is presided over by the magnificent Shwe Dagon Pagoda – an overpowering reminder of the importance of Buddhism in Burmese life.

Previous page:
The older a Burmese woman gets, the more fussy she becomes about her cheroot. Most insist on rolling their own, and they like to pack in as much tobacco as possible. It is not uncommon to see ancient, toothless crones sucking away at enormous rolls of tobacco wrapped in newspaper or maize leaves.

The Irrawaddy is navigable for most of its length and provides the chief link between northern and southern Burma. On the other hand, there is only one bridge across it – just south of Mandalay – so that the river effectively splits the eastern and western halves of the country. Here, a cargo of bamboo has been made into a raft, which can carry a further cargo of pottery – thus doubling the profits of a long journey at the pace of the current if travelling down river, or at the even slower pace of the oarsmen if travelling up river.

The Land of a Hundred Thousand Pagodas

The air is clammy with humidity. Fans add their hum to the patter of the rain, without managing to stir even the gentlest of breezes. From outside come bursts of noise: people's laughs and cries, mingled with the gurgling of a waterspout. In the street, people are sheltering as best they can from the downpour. Three or four squeeze under one of the big black umbrellas that are used as shelter from the sun as often as from the rain. Others roll up their *longyis*, the sarong-like skirts worn by both men and women – to little avail. The street by now is a torrent of running water and the market-place at the foot of the slope a quagmire. But who cares? The Burmese are always happy to see the rain. It makes the rice swell and vegetables grow.

Rangoon's lush vegetation bends under the weight of water, and any roaming animals go to ground. Then, as suddenly as it started, the rain ceases and all is transformed. The birds resume their singing, followed by the whirring of insects. Scavenging dogs bark as they contest a few scraps of food. Above the vivid green tree tops, crows flap their way across a clear sky that has regained its azure brilliance. In this way, Burmese life adjusts its pace for five months every year – from May to October – to the comings and goings of the monsoon rains.

Well protected from its neighbours – India, Bangladesh, China, Laos and Thailand – by the natural defences of rivers and mountains, Burma has kept itself to itself for several decades. It won independence from Britain in 1948, thanks in large part to the leadership of the nationalist hero Aung San – assassinated before independence took effect. It then followed a turbulent course until, in 1962, a military coup was followed by the establishment of a new Socialist Republic of the Union of Burma. Since then the army has stayed firmly in the saddle, in spite of growing opposition led by, among others, Aung San's daughter. While their human rights record leaves much to be desired, the government's policy of keeping the country isolated from the outside world has allowed Burma's traditions to remain largely intact. Nor has it done much to disturb the Buddhist religion. Almost 90 per cent of Burmese are Buddhists, and evidence of their faith abounds; there is hardly a hill, cave, cliff, spring or village without its pagoda or *stupa* (a Buddhist centre of worship) dominating the surrounding countryside.

Burmese landscapes

The sun setting over the crisscrossing waterways of the Irrawaddy delta reveals one of Burma's most magical landscapes – best enjoyed, if you can arrange it, from one of the heavy dinghies known as sampans. Lining the banks on either side of you are groves of breadfruit, mango and guava trees, all heavy with fruit in season. Beyond them are glimpses of rice paddies, threshing floors, bamboo thickets and groups of palm trees, with a few small houses sheltering beneath them.

At the rear of the craft, the sampan's oarsman stands silhouetted against the rapidly darkening sky. All is still, apart from the gentle plashing of his one oar with which he both propels and steers the craft, and the sound of the small, rippling waves of the rising tide as they break against the hull. It is the time of day when water buffaloes come down to wallow up to their necks in the stream or roll contentedly in the mud. The men leave their small square fields – light or dark green or golden brown, according to the season – and start to make their way home. Women and children who have come to replenish the family's water supplies take the opportunity for a cooling dip, and splash one another with happy abandon.

The Irrawaddy is more than just a line of communication. It is also important as a source of water for irrigation and for the fertile silt it leaves behind after the monsoon floods. People come to the Irrawaddy to bathe, to do their washing, to fetch water for the home, and to sell whatever they can to travellers on the various river boats that ply its length. The women here are pounding cloves of garlic, which they will then mix with fish paste and pepper and fry to make the popular snack, ngapi.

A cigar-smoking fisherman paddles across the waters of Lake Inle, on the Shan Plateau. The lake is mostly shallow and fish are abundant, allowing the locals to practise one of the simplest methods imaginable for catching them. A fisherman keeps a close eye on the bed of the lake as he makes his way across it. When he spots a shoal of fish, he simply drops his long, tubular net into the midst of it. He can then pull out by hand as many fish as he wants.

Light canoe-like craft such as these are the standard means of transport on Lake Inle. People use them to navigate the 'streets' of the lake villages, to go to the floating market and to get to their floating vegetable patches. Slipping silently through the waters, they make a pleasant contrast with the noisy 'put-put' of the motor boats used for longer trips.

But this is just one of Burma's landscapes. Take the little train from Thazi to Kalaw, far to the north in central Burma, and you find yourself in another world altogether. All around is a plain swept by hot, dry winds with almost desert-like vegetation growing on it: cactuses and sugar palms, with cotton, sesame and peanuts as the chief crops. Sand dunes and rocky gullies (*chaungs*) – which in the monsoon season suddenly turn into raging torrents – give the scenery a distinctly lunar aspect, particularly at night. Then, on the horizon, rises the jagged escarpment of the Shan Plateau. Here, all changes yet again. Forests, dominated by the huge, pillar-like boles of teak trees, spread out on either side, while the undergrowth is formed by tree ferns and splashed with brilliant-hued jacaranda blossoms and flame-coloured poincianas. As you penetrate deeper into the plateau, the vegetation becomes thicker until it forms a dense jungle, the realm of tigers, elephants and boars. Burma's 3 million Shan tribespeople also live on the plateau, traditionally by slash-and-burn agriculture, though in recent years the opium trade of the infamous Golden Triangle (much of which falls within the Shan State) has presented an alternative source of income. There are Shan armies fighting for independence from Rangoon which the Burmese army has been unable to crush.

Returning to Rangoon by plane you are able to take in the three principal constituents of the Burmese landscape: thick forests and jungles, bone-dry plains and flooded rice paddies. As for Rangoon itself, the Burmese capital – almost all of its buildings dating from the time of the Raj, and almost all of them in an advanced state of decrepitude – has a down-at-heel charm. In 1991, in an attempt to smarten up the capital, many of the buildings were repainted, and the government imposed penalties for not repainting.

Sited on a bend on the Hlaing river, Rangoon boasts lakes and parks where families and lovers come to take the air or have dinner in one of the outdoor restaurants

that flourish there in the dry season. Elsewhere, life is lived cheek by jowl in the city's various districts: the Indian quarter, with a busy market and all-pervading smell of hot spices; the Chinese quarter, generally most active after dark; and the slightly smarter administrative centre. Thanks to Burma's international isolation, the port area is less busy than it once was, but it too retains its charm: it is a mass of sampans and river steamers, with gulls wailing overhead, waiting to pounce on some forgotten scrap of fish or bread.

But, above all, Rangoon is dominated by the great Shwe Dagon Pagoda – 'a beautiful, winking wonder' as Rudyard Kipling described it. Its domed and gilded central *stupa* is set on a small hill and rises in all some 1000 feet above sea level. It is quite unmistakable. The outside of the *stupa* is covered with 8688 slabs of solid

The principles of roofing a Burmese house could hardly be simpler. Palm leaves are cut, dried in the sun, sorted according to length and attached to a piece of bamboo. All that needs to be done then is to lay them out across the roof and fasten them down, making sure that the different layers overlap one another. How long the roof lasts depends on how well the leaves were prepared and the thickness of the layers, but one that has been well laid should last five years or so. Mutual help is, of course, crucial and widely practised, the whole village turning out to help one family roof their home.

The Inthas – the name means 'Sons of the Lake' – get around Lake Inle by the ingenious use of leg power. Their boats have platforms at the front and back, on which they balance themselves with one leg, using the other to manoeuvre the long, pole-like oar. Boys are taught the knack from an early age, though women generally make do with an ordinary paddle.

The breadfruit comes from the same family as the mulberry, but could hardly be more different. It produces large, heavy fruits – the size of a grapefruit or bigger – with a starchy, white or yellowish flesh. Since a single tree can yield 800 fruits in one season, it is a highly useful food source.

gold; set into its tip are 2317 rubies, sapphires and topazes and 5448 diamonds. Around it is a huge terrace with more than 100 lesser *stupas,* shrines, halls and pavilions, reached by four stairways, one at each point of the compass. The site has been regarded as holy for more than 2000 years and every passing group has left its mark: temples and pagodas built by Indian, Chinese and Nepalese immigrants, countless statues of Buddha, and huge, gold-plated bells weighing up to 40 tons.

Every day, thousands of worshippers, pilgrims and tourists troop through the Shwe Dagon. Some break away from the crowd to seek the shade of an old banyan tree, where they either drowse or meditate the time away. Others pray more busily at the various shrines dedicated to the days of the week; according to Burmese astrology, the day of the week you were born on has an important influence on your life. Each day has its symbolic animal, indicative of the kind of influence it exerts. Sunday is represented by the mythical galon or garuda bird; Monday by the tiger;

Tuesday by the lion. Wednesday is divided into two: the period from midnight to noon is represented by the tusked elephant; from noon to the following midnight by the tuskless elephant. Thursday is represented by the rat; Friday by the guinea pig; and Saturday by the serpent.

Elsewhere in the pagoda enclosure, worshippers and priests go about their affairs. Some of the lesser *stupas* are covered in bamboo scaffolding, usually a sign that

To own a pair of buffaloes is wealth indeed in Burma. Buffaloes are used to plough the rice paddies and pull carts, the most common form of transport in the countryside. They are good-natured beasts, whose most exquisite pleasure is to submerge themselves up to their necks in cool water or to wallow in the mud.

The water hyacinth, although it has attractive blue flowers, has become a pest. It spreads quickly and is almost impossible to root out. It is common in stagnant water where it does at least act as a filter to help to purify the water. But along the shores of Lake Inle, among other places, it is a serious nuisance that clogs up the various waterways.

regilding is in process. A group of women, dressed in penitential brown, gather round a monk to receive his teaching. And through it all, incense mingles with the scent of frangipani flowers, which grows stronger and more intoxicating as the day draws to its close. Finally, as night falls, the great central *stupa* gleams majestically in the sun's last rays.

Presenting a different scene, is the Bahan bazaar, at the foot of the Shwe Dagon's eastern stairway. Here,

stalls offer flowers, sticks of incense, gold leaf (which pilgrims paste on to the *stupas*), sandalwood, parasols and richly clothed wooden puppets – any browser who examines the puppets beneath their robes will discover that the differences of gender have not been forgotten. Burma's craft traditions are represented in bronze bells and gongs, drums, knives, lacquerware, sculptures, musical instruments and toys. Bookbinders ply their trade, and at the lower end of the market are shops that

Burma used to be the world's biggest exporter of rice, and still ranks seventh. The rice is cultivated in a six-month cycle, starting in June and ending in December. The women here are planting out young rice plants that have previously been growing in nursery beds.

This substantial house from the Mandalay region is typical of the comfortable dwellings that many better-off Burmese build for themselves. In this case, the pilings on which the house is built have been covered over with walls of plaited bamboo stems. The resulting ground storey, with an earth floor, is used as a storeroom and workshop. The living quarters are on the first floor. The wood and bamboo building materials provide a much-needed natural insulation in a region where the summer heat can be suffocating.

specialise in monastic clothing. Scattered throughout the pagoda's precincts are food stalls offering sweet and savoury snacks.

Calendars and kitsch

Traditional Burmese houses are raised on pilings, since the monsoon downpours can raise water levels by a foot or more within a few hours, causing widespread flooding. Building houses on stilts also allows air to circulate more freely through them, keeping the rooms fresh and cool.

These houses are made almost entirely from natural materials (though corrugated iron is now as ubiquitous in Burma as it is in most developing countries). Bamboo is the cheapest and most popular building material, with some hard woods (mostly teak) used as well. Floorboards generally consist of lengths of bamboo tied loosely together. The gaps between them again allow the air to circulate freely and also permit people in the

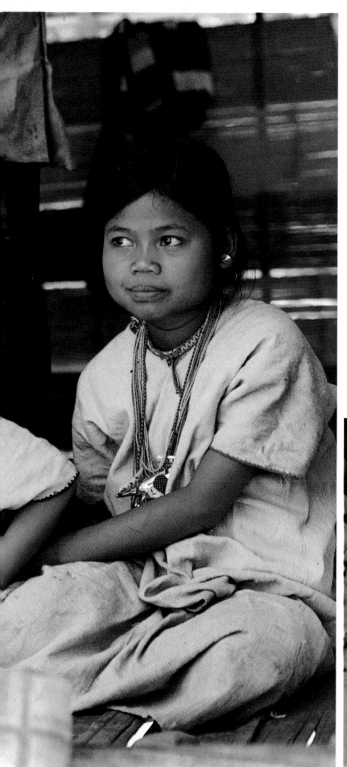

The 2 to 3 million Karens living in Burma are one of the country's most important tribal minorities. They have their own Karen State, but only about a third of them live there. Many prefer Rangoon, where they tend to work as servants or in the hospitals. The women, as here, wear long tunics, white for girls, black once they are married. Unlike most of the country's other peoples, the majority of Karens are Christians, having been converted in the 19th century by British missionaries.

Burmese wood carvers are heirs of an ancient tradition. It was their predecessors, for example, who created the wonderfully sculpted gable ends that adorn so many Buddhist monasteries. Some of the finest specimens of their art are the carved teak panels of the former royal palace of Mandalay. The palace was destroyed in the Second World War, except for one of its buildings, moved outside the palace grounds by King Thibaw, and is now known as the Shwenandaw Monastery.

Leaves are put to many uses in Burma. They can be used to wrap up your midday meal if you are going to be away from home, and then unfurled and used as a plate, as here. Larger leaves make handy and surprisingly effective umbrellas and parasols, too.

house to do without a dustbin; they simply throw their rubbish, mostly odds and ends of food, through the gaps in the floor and let the various hens, ducks and pigs below devour it all.

The walls are made from woven bamboo stems which the Burmese with their natural love of decoration usually arrange so that the darker stems alternate with the lighter ones. Roofs are thatched, using matted grasses, teak or palm leaves or woven bamboo, depending on the region.

A bamboo staircase leads to the multi-purpose main room, where the family eat, talk and entertain during the day and some sleep at night. The furniture is very simple: a few mats on the floor; some thin, hard mattresses which act as beds at night and are rolled up during the day; a low table with a pot of hot green tea

always standing ready; a few shelves; and an ancient radio, permanently switched on, usually at full blast. Better-off families may have a glass-fronted cabinet and a few clocks.

Another decorative detail rarely missing from Burmese homes is the colourful array of calendars. These come in all shapes and sizes: calendars put out by airlines with glossy photographs showing the wonders of far-off lands; calendars from one of the few foreign companies that operate in Burma; Chinese calendars, originating from both Communist China and Taiwan; Thai calendars; even some local Burmese calendars. Many of them will be out of date, but this does not matter. No one would ever dream of taking them down. They hang there as a witness to the Burmese people's curiosity about foreign countries (not just Western ones), and as one of the few available links they have with the outside world.

The final essential element in the home is the family altar, often in a distinctly kitsch style. At their most sober, these east-facing shrines consist of no more than a statue of the Buddha in alabaster, bronze or gilded wood placed on a chest. More often it is surrounded by plastic flowers and artificial wreaths in garish shades of yellow, pink and green. A neon tube or strings of small

The Burmese are extremely clean people, who wash at least twice a day, if not more. They also like to change their clothes regularly. Even the poorest people possess at least two sarong-like longyis, *and shirts, to allow them to change every day. These bathers are splashing themselves in the warm waters of Lake Inle.*

flashing bulbs (similar to those used on Christmas trees in the West) illuminate the scene. There may also be gaudily painted images of the 37 *nats*, pre-Buddhist nature spirits that are still widely worshipped in Burma, while in front of the altar are offerings of fresh fruit (bananas, oranges and mangoes), cooked rice and heavily scented flowers, all of which are renewed every day.

As for the rest of the home: parents in search of privacy usually partition off a corner of the main room with bamboo screens. In lowland regions, the kitchen is attached to the house at the back; in mountain areas, it is more often a separate building. On the Shan Plateau, one tribe, the 5000-strong Palaungs, live in long collective houses, which will extend as far as the lie of the land permits. Some have as many as ten different households living under a single roof.

Monastic living

Buddhism permeates Burmese life through and through. Every village has its monastery, and Buddhist monks (*pongyi*) dominated the country's education system until the British introduced mission schools and state schools towards the end of the 19th century. They still offer many poor children the best chance they have of getting a decent schooling. It is hard to give an exact figure for how many monks there are in Burma, because many ordinary people adopt the monastic robes and way of life for a few months as an act of devotion. They then

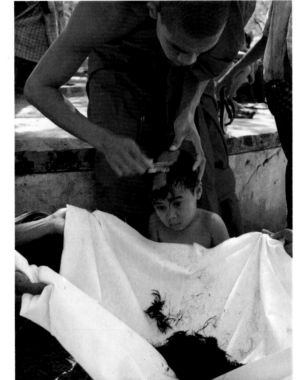

When he left his father's palace, the young Siddhartha Gautama, the future Buddha, shaved off all his hair as a sign that he was renouncing his old life. Burmese monks continue the practice in a special ceremony when young novices enter the monastery.

Water is precious, particularly in the dry regions of central Burma. Here, the barrel-like containers of water carts are being filled at a small reservoir – they will then distribute the water to the local households. Such services are provided free by the local authorities, or sometimes subsidised by rich local merchants.

return to normal life. Probably there are 120,000 full-time monks in a total population of more than 37.5 million people.

Usually the monastery, built like a family house on high pilings, but with an ornately carved teak roof that few homes can match, is by far the most impressive building in a village. You enter it barefooted – as a mark of respect – and few visitors fail to be impressed by the sense of peace and serenity inside. All around, in the large shady rooms, is a motley collection of clocks, thrones of gilded wood, statues and offerings left by the faithful. Some monastic communities are particularly impressive. Rising from the banks of the Irrawaddy near Mandalay in central Burma is the hill of Sagaing. Here, no fewer than 5000 monks and nuns live in 100 or so separate communities scattered over the hillside. Some of the buildings are imposing, a few of them looking like down-at-heel Venetian palaces. During the daytime, the entire hill is dotted with the orange splashes of the monks' robes and the pink ones of the nuns.

Every year Sagaing is the setting for one of Burma's most colourful festivals. Its roots lie in the tradition that the *Sangha* (monastic community) and its members should live by begging, and in most communities the

The sun is already high in the sky and a group of monks are returning from their daily quest for food. They are carrying all that they are allowed to own: their orange robes, a fan (used to help them to concentrate when meditating, but here fending off the sun's rays), a black lacquerware begging bowl and a bag containing a few personal items, such as a razor and a strainer to make sure they never swallow a living thing.

monks do indeed file out solemnly at dawn each morning to seek their daily bread and other necessities. The problem at Sagaing is that there are too many monks and nuns for the local towns and villages to support. As a result, collections are organised throughout Burma for the Sagaing *pongyi*. Once a year the gifts are gathered together and taken first to Mandalay, where the occasion is an excuse for

having no possessions. But they are devout in other ways. People will travel miles on foot to listen to the teachings of a well-respected monk or to take part in the annual festival of a pagoda. Many also make a habit of carrying out meritorious acts, which they believe will help to free them from the wheel of existence and enable their souls to reach the paradise of Nirvana after death – rather than being endlessly reincarnated. For

In a country where everything has to be repaired and nothing is ever thrown away, the blacksmith has an important role. Here, a village blacksmith is shaping the iron band that goes around the wheel of an ox cart. He has to be able to make and mend all kinds of implements and gadgets, for such things are rarely available ready-made.

celebrations. Barges filled with rice and the other offerings then move downstream to Sagaing, where the *pongyi* await them. By tradition, the task of distributing the gifts is given to the head of one of the communities of nuns. Also by tradition, she allots more rice per head to the male communities than to the female ones – though a few more free-thinking nuns have challenged this rule in recent years.

The high esteem Burmese people generally have for their monks and nuns is a reflection of their respect for the Buddhist faith as a whole. Ordinary Burmese do not feel obliged to follow the strict way of life of the *pongyi* – whose rules include not eating after midday and

one person this might involve fasting once a week; for another never refusing to give a beggar money; for another spending part of his free time helping to build a new temple, or repair an old one.

It is an approach to life that seems to give them a remarkable vitality and gaiety, which can be seen in all areas of living, including the most practical. The Burmese inhabit one of the poorest countries in Asia where the few foreign goods that appear are almost all reserved for privileged sectors of society, such as the military. Maintaining the simplest form of machinery in such conditions can be a nightmare, yet somehow the Burmese make do, using a few bits and pieces of bamboo and wire and plenty of good humour. The same relaxed approach can be seen in the upbringing of children. It is rare to see parents smacking or berating their children, who are generally well behaved without such measures. Burma is also one of the few countries in South-East Asia where it is common to see young couples walking along the street hand in hand.

The road to Mandalay

People wake early in Mandalay, Burma's second city and, in the eyes of many, its intellectual, artistic and religious heart. At five o'clock on a cool, dark, winter's morning, the streets are already busy with well-muffled figures making their way to work. Here and there, large cooking pots are steaming away over charcoal fires. Gathered round them are groups of bicycle-rickshaw drivers, most of whom have spent the night curled up as best they can inside their bicycle rickshaws.

Presiding over one fire is the plump, reassuring figure of Daw Sein, who makes a meagre living by selling *mohinga*, a soup of noodles mixed with fish paste and aromatic herbs. Daw is a name given to older women as a sign of respect, and Daw Sein is certainly a stately presence. Her hair is still thick and glossy and, like most other Burmese women, she wears it in a heavy, round bun wrapped around a wooden comb on the nape of her neck. Coating her face and arms is a yellow powder known as *thanatka*, which acts as a kind of natural suntan lotion; it will protect her skin from the savage burning of the sun later in the day. Daw Sein simply daubs the *thanatka* on, but younger, more coquettish women use the powder as a form of make-up and even draw leaves and flowers on their cheeks with it.

Taking a break from handing out the bowls of *mohinga*, Daw Sein lights her first cheroot of the day. In this, too, she is typical of her nation. Kipling's Tommy soldier in his poem 'The Road to Mandalay' describes how he first saw his Burmese love 'a-smokin' of a whackin' white cheroot', and the Burmese have remained heavy smokers to this day – none more so than the older women like Daw Sein. Wherever you go in the country, you see them puffing away at their huge cheroots (the size of a large cigar), usually with a small pan at the ready. The pan is an important precaution. The cheaper cheroots consist almost as much of stems as of leaves of tobacco; as the women draw on the cheroot they hold the pan under it to catch any burning fragments that fall off.

Dawn begins to break and the city settles down to its daily routine. This involves a good deal of leisure as well as work, and in the open spaces where streets meet, groups of young men gather to play the Burmese national game, *chinlon*. Standing inside a circle, usually slightly more than 20 feet across, they pass a hollow, wickerwork ball between them, patting it with feet, legs, head, shoulders – any part of the body, in fact, except the hands and arms.

The hours pass, and soon it is time for the midday meal. This is an important part of the day for the Burmese, for whom the soups and noodle dishes sold at

The market at Taunggyi, the capital of the Shan State, is famous for its rich arrays of vegetable produce and for all the different ethnic groups you see there, dressed in their tribal finery. There is also a night market, chiefly known for illicit deals between locals and smugglers bringing much-prized consumer goods from Thailand.

The Paos are one of the many small tribes of the Shan State. Men and women alike wear simple black tunics, with jewellery and turbans providing a more colourful note. The Paos also use the longyi, *though not always as a garment. This woman is using hers to carry her baby on her back.*

The crumbling but still magnificent façade of a Victorian building in Rangoon. The capital's hot and humid climate – it has an average annual rainfall of nearly 100 inches – is hard on its buildings, whose stonework is constantly being eroded as a result. The city has an air of decaying, if rather endearing, splendour.

streetside stalls are no more than snacks to keep them going. The main meal consists of a plate piled high with steaming rice and accompanied by a curry, a soup (usually clear and with a sharp, tangy flavour) and some raw vegetables. The curries are often delicious, made from fish, prawns, pork, beef and chicken, though a few of the regional variations can seem less appetising to Western visitors: the specialities of the Mon tribespeople of southern Burma, for instance, are dog curry and monkey curry.

After the meal, people settle back for some *lapet*. This is a delicacy consisting of pickled tea leaves. Traditionally, it is kept in a lacquer box along with some fried garlic, toasted sesame seeds and peanuts, and various pulses. You pick out a pinch of each with the tips of your fingers, put it all in your mouth, rinse your fingers in a waterbowl, then wash it all down with some ordinary liquid tea. The whole concoction leaves a sharp, refreshing flavour in the mouth.

Rice farmers, palm farmers and the art of lacquerware

Among the chief beneficiaries of the 1962 revolution were the peasant rice farmers of the Irrawaddy delta. Land reforms following the revolution gave them back much of the land they had lost over the years to the *chettyars*, moneylenders from southern India who had settled in Burma during the British Raj.

The rice they produce is among the best in the world. It is a long-grained variety, planted and harvested in a six-monthly cycle (the Burmese have a marked aversion to faster-growing rices which, they say, create too much work and in any case leave you feeling hungry only a couple of hours after you have eaten). In some families one member earns a little extra income by ferrying people across the delta's maze of waterways in a sampan, but for much of the year, especially during the monsoon season and when the rice is being planted and harvested, there is enough work to keep everyone busy in the paddies. Once harvested, the rice is taken in long trains of ox-drawn wagons to the local mill – an evocative sight from another age, with the wagons rolling along at the steady pace of the hump-backed oxen, and the whole procession shrouded in a cloud of fine dust. At the mill, the rice is husked and polished and then transported to the towns and villages of the rest of Burma.

Pagan at the heart of the semi-desert flatlands of central Burma presents a different picture. Here, the peasant makes his living by extracting the sap of the palm trees that abound in the region; the sap is made into an alcoholic drink or sweet syrup. It is hard work, which involves shinning up each palm (most peasants 'farm' around 40 trees) at least twice a day and slashing the flower buds to let out the precious liquid. To complicate matters, the system of ownership is extremely complex. Few farmers own their trees and even the owners of the trees do not necessarily own the land they grow on . . . In spite of all these difficulties the whole process carries on, satisfactorily enough, year in, year out.

The Pagan region is best known for its lacquerware, which has experienced a boom over the last ten years as the Burmese authorities have tentatively opened the door to tourism. It is an ancient craft, requiring an innate artistic sense as well as sound organisation, and is still carried out in small family workshops. They produce everything from bowls, plates, cigar boxes and coffee sets, to ritual dishes used to present offerings in the temples, chests, small tables and screens – all presenting glorious patterns of rich colour and gold leaf. There is no question of mass production here. A minimum of two months is needed to make even the simplest coffee service, and something more ambitious like a screen may take up to 18 months. Despite the popularity of lacquerware with tourists, local Burmese are still its biggest buyers. Pious donors, for example, make sure that every monk has his plain black lacquerware bowl for alms food.

Religion also provides the chief market for many of Burma's other craftsmen. Among these are Mandalay's alabaster sculptors, who do the bulk of their business making statues of the Buddha, as well as some tombstones for the local Chinese community. They are organised into professional studios, where everyone has his place according to his experience and skill. When new blocks of alabaster arrive, it is the apprentices who go to work on them first, leaving the rough outlines of a head and body. More experienced craftsmen then take over, carving in the details of the body and clothing, but not touching the head. This task is left exclusively for the master sculptor, so that at any time there will be rows of half-finished Buddhas sitting in the studio courtyard waiting for the master to touch them into life. The final stage is usually performed by women who polish the sculptures with pebbles gathered from the Irrawaddy to give them their characteristic milky white finish.

Another skilled craft is that of making the gold leaf that Burmese people use to gild their *stupas* and statues of the Buddha as an act of devotion. This, like the lacquerware business, is organised around family workshops. They are divided into two groups. First, the 'beaters' receive the gold in small slabs which they place between two sheets of lightly oiled rice paper and then wrap in leather. After that, they beat it with heavy hammers so that the gold softens slightly and spreads out between the leaves of rice paper. Next, the gold is sent to another workshop, which is sealed against any kind of draught that could disturb the fragile leaf. Teams of girls sitting cross-legged on the floor cut each portion of gold into four and then send it back to the beaters. And so the process goes on until the gold is transformed into an almost cobweb-like texture. It is then sold to the faithful at the entrances to pagodas, along with flowers and sticks of incense. The amount of gold applied in some holy places is remarkable. The statue of Buddha in Mandalay's great Maha Myat Muni Pagoda, for instance, has acquired an outer skin of gold leaf at least eight inches thick, and every year the monks in charge of the pagoda sweep up several pounds of gold that has dropped to the floor.

Another important craft is jewellery. The Burmese like to adorn themselves, and their jewellers have been regarded as among the most skilled in Asia. Burma, especially the Mogok region north-east of Mandalay, is rich in gemstones, and this has led to a problem with smuggling. As a result, Mogok is now closed to everyone (including any Burmese) who does not live there. Many tourists who come back gleefully from a Burmese bazaar bearing a magnificent-looking ruby they have exchanged for a bottle of Western perfume would be shocked to discover the truth: that Burma imports large quantities of synthetic rubies from Europe.

Floating gardens on Lake Inle

The Shan State boasts a gem of a different kind: Lake Inle, spreading out to the south of the former British hill station of Taunggyi, more than 3000 feet above sea level. The lake, which covers some 60 square miles, is home to yet another of Burma's tribal peoples, the Inthas or 'Sons of the Lake', who live in villages actually on the lake. Their houses are raised on stilts a few yards out from the shore, many of them imposing, two-storey structures built of teak.

The Inthas use small boats, propelled and steered by a single oar for getting from house to house within a

The bicycle rickshaw is by far the most popular means of transport in the towns and cities. The passenger seat is usually at the side, rather than the rear, and when there are two passengers they travel back to back. For many people, from students to unemployed workers, driving a rickshaw is an excellent means of earning quick money. This driver is delivering a colourful cargo of cushions.

village; larger craft for going out fishing; and a few with outboard motors for longer journeys across the lake. The smaller boats for local use are the most numerous – you need one for even the most basic purposes, such as going to the toilet, which generally consists of a small cabin-like building rising from its stilts at a short distance from the village. The fishing boats, meanwhile, are most remarkable for the way in which the Inthas

manoeuvre them. Rather like punts, they have a flat ledge fore and aft. The fisherman perches with one leg on the ledge, while he wraps his other leg around the oar to manipulate it. From this position, he is better able to peer into the waters of the lake looking for fish (Inle is mostly shallow and its waters clear, so that this method of operating is perfectly feasible), and his hands are free to deal with his fishing nets.

Cheroots are made throughout Burma and there are numerous brands. Making them is a simple process: the tobacco leaves and stems are roughly chopped and then rolled up inside an outer leaf. They are fitted with a roll made from dried maize leaves to act as a filter. When smoked, they give off the acrid smell that is so characteristic of the country. Cheroot makers like this girl earn only a few kyats (the lowest unit of the Burmese currency) a day, but at least the work is regular.

This woman is carefully polishing a statue of Buddha, made from alabaster quarried in the hills near Mandalay. For the task, she uses different grades of pebbles fished from the Irrawaddy. First of all, she rubs it with coarse pebbles, then with finer ones and lastly with sand. Her work will be finished only when the surface of the statue is smooth and milky white. It all takes several hours, but fortunately patience is one commodity that is never in short supply in Burma.

Fishing is the principal occupation of the Intha men – the women are Burma's only silk weavers. The lower storeys of their houses are generally given over to large, airy workshops where they produce, among other things, the silk *longyis* for which Inle is famous. They also make the finely woven Shan shoulder bags used by children throughout Burma as satchels and by men for carrying their gear from place to place. Unfortunately, few of these workshops are operating now to full capacity as they depend on the government for supplies of raw silk, which frequently runs out. None the less, they help to make the 70,000-odd Inthas one of Burma's wealthiest tribal peoples.

As well as fishing and weaving, the lake people have a third speciality: their *kyun-myaw* or floating gardens. An Intha who wants to do a bit of gardening takes some of the water weeds and tows them back home or to wherever he wants to anchor his garden. He can enlarge it by adding further patches until he ends up with something the size of a football pitch. Alternatively, he can make his own garden. To do this, he takes some of the water weeds that clog the shores of the lake and the streams and rivers flowing into it, and ties them together into bunches to form a kind of raft. He then dredges up some of the fertile silt from the bottom of the lake and spreads it out over the weed-raft . . . and he has his floating garden. In this way, the Inthas produce most of the tomatoes eaten in Burma, as well as rich crops of beans, peas, cabbages, cauliflowers and other vegetables and flowers. It is with some justice that they claim that the lake nourishes them.

Not surprisingly, the lake is also the setting for their principal festivals. The most spectacular of these takes place in September when five golden statues of the Buddha, normally housed in Inle's Phaung Daw U Pagoda, are carried on a gilded barge around the lake's chief villages. The festival's other great event is the leg-rowing contests, when oarsmen using the traditional method of propelling their craft challenge each other to races across short stretches of water. Inthas and outsiders alike gather in great excitement for the races,

which have a unique magic – testifying, apart from anything else, to the admirable harmony between the Intha people and their environment.

Burma's river artery

Another great waterway, the 1250-mile-long Irrawaddy, also sustains its own characteristic patterns of life. Cutting its way through the country from north to south and, astonishingly, crossed by only a single bridge, British-built, to the south of Mandalay, it is one of the chief means of transporting both people and merchandise from one end of the country to the other. Among its most striking sights are the great floating trains of teak logs, felled in the forests of the north, which can take up to two months on their journey downstream. To assure their comfort for the period, the

Several families in Mandalay make their living by producing the gold leaf that the Burmese like to use to adorn their stupas and images of the Buddha. Women and girls such as these spend eight hours a day cutting out the leaf, while their menfolk beat it down to the correct thickness. It is a suffocating task, for the slightest breath of air will send the fragile leaf flying – consequently, there is no ventilation in the workshops.

Yoke Thay puppets are still very popular in central Burma. They first appeared in the early 16th century and were hugely successful – to the extent that many Burmese dances are based on the stiff gestures of the puppets. The puppet master has to be both strong (each puppet weighs several pounds) and dextrous – some are manipulated with up to 60 different strings. Yoke Thay troupes have 28 puppets; there is also a small orchestra. The shows tell stories from the early life of Buddha and Burmese folk tales.

men in charge of them lash the logs into crude rafts and build a few huts on top of these vast structures.

When they reach Mandalay, most of the logs are hauled out of the water and taken to the local timber mills. Teams of buffaloes, some pushing, the others pulling, heave the great pieces of timber ashore and on to ancient trucks. This sight, too, has its beauty: the splashing of men and beasts, the loud cries of encouragement, the harsher 'thwack' of drivers beating their animals, the relief when the logs finally fall into place on the trucks. In its combination of tenacity, ingenuity and agility, it is a typically Burmese scene, symbolic of the adaptability that has enabled the people to survive their turbulent history with so much good humour.

Travelling about 100 miles downstream from Mandalay the Irrawaddy passes Pagan, which was the capital of Burma between 1044 and 1287. The ancient city – which sprawls across some six square miles – was once a leading centre of Buddhist learning and hundreds of *stupas* still dot the banks of the Irrawaddy. Many of the monuments, and some larger temples, were devastated by an earthquake in 1975 but the ruined city remains an important site on any tourist itinerary.

Asia's forgotten land

Burma's tourist industry is one of the least developed in Asia. This is largely because the government's isolationist policies have, for decades, discouraged tourism; until the late 1980s visitors were only allowed into the country for a week at a time. Ethnic conflict in many parts of the country makes it dangerous to travel 'off-limits' – outside the official tourist routes – so large parts of the country remain almost undiscovered by travellers.

Although a more vigorous tourist industry would have generated much-needed hard currency, it would undoubtedly have brought some of the negative aspects that characterise some other countries in the region – commercialism and rising crime, for example. It is almost certainly because Burma has been isolated for so long that the country and its people have retained so much of their natural charm.

The kye-waing *is the gong section of a Burmese orchestra. The player sits at the centre with his instruments around him in a circle, all of them richly carved, painted and gilded. The other orchestral instruments are drums, bamboo xylophones, flutes and oboes, cymbals and clappers, and a spectacular set of 21 tuned drums arranged in a circle. The only stringed instrument is a boat-shaped harp.*

Gazetteer

India

The republic of India is the second most populous country in the world; only China has more people. About 14 major languages and hundreds of dialects are spoken in India. Nearly 84 per cent of the population are Hindu in religion. In addition, the Muslim population, about 10 per cent, makes India the world's third largest Islamic nation.

The country today is smaller than in the days of British rule. When Britain granted independence to the peoples of its Indian empire in 1947, power was transferred to two successor states and the country was partitioned between them. The predominantly Muslim areas took the name of Pakistan; while the Hindu-dominated remainder kept the name of India.

Indian society is a sometimes uneasy mixture of East and West – the natural consequence of a meeting between a civilisation which in many basic ways has changed little in 2000 years, and the ideas and beliefs of foreign conquerors. Though vast new industries are being developed, life in many parts of India still moves at the leisurely pace of the ox cart.

Aryan invasions

From c. 2000 BC onwards, invaders known as Aryans

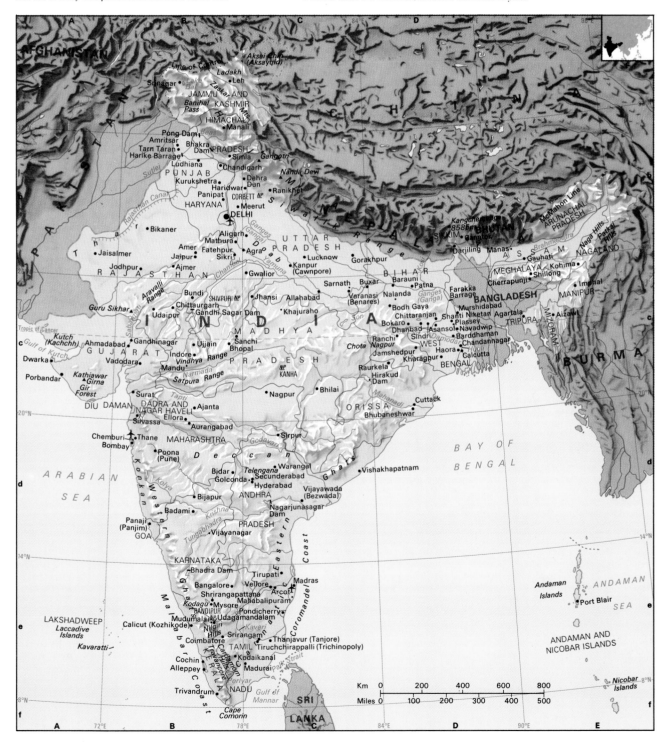

INDIA AT A GLANCE

Area 1,261,816 square miles
Population 843,931,000
Capital Delhi
Government Federal republic
Currency Rupee = 100 paisa
Languages Hindi and English official, but at least 13 other languages used including Urdu
Religions Hindu (83%), Muslim (10%), Christian (3%), Sikh (2%), Buddhist (1%), Jain (1%)
Climate Tropical; monsoon from June to September. Average temperature in New Delhi ranges from 7-21°C (45-70°F) in January to 26-41°C (79-106°F) in May
Main primary products Rice, wheat, sugar cane, barley, sorghum, millet, potatoes, tea, groundnuts, cotton, jute, pulses, vegetables, fruit; coal, iron ore, oil and gas, bauxite, chromite, copper, manganese, gemstones
Major industries Textiles, iron and steel, transport equipment, chemicals, fertilisers, machinery, oil refining, agriculture, cement, coke, food processing, beverages
Main exports Textiles, food (including fish, tea), machinery, gemstones, iron ore, leather
Annual income per head (US$) 400
Population growth (per thous/yr) 21
Life expectancy (yrs) Male 52 **Female** 53

descended upon India through the mountain passes of the north-west, establishing themselves in the Punjab and on the plains of the Ganges. The Aryans absorbed a sophisticated civilisation already existing in the Indus valley; and they introduced to India the forerunner of many of its present languages. Knowledge of the Aryans comes mainly from their four great religious books, the Vedas, which were the first holy books of Hinduism.

The Aryans were divided into three social classes: warriors, priests and common people. On settling in India, they added a fourth class, the conquered. From this simple division between conqueror and conquered, between light-skinned Aryan and dark-skinned non-Aryan, India's immensely complicated social system of caste developed.

Foundation of the Maurya Empire
Invasion again struck India from the north-west in 327 BC when Alexander the Great marched through the Khyber Pass, bent on conquering the subcontinent. His armies were eventually driven out by the founder of the Maurya Empire, Chandragupta (c. 322-298 BC).

The greatest Maurya ruler was Asoka (273-232 BC). After a period of bloody conquest which brought the whole of India, except for its southern tip, under his rule Asoka was converted to Buddhism. He reorganised the state on humane lines, renounced war and encouraged the spread of Buddhist principles.

Golden age of the Guptas
In the 4th century AD, a new dynasty, that of the Guptas (named after the Maurya emperor, Chandragupta), spread over northern India. This dynasty held power for more than a century. It nurtured a revival of the Hindu religion and a golden age in Hindu art and literature, which carried on after the collapse of the Guptas under the attacks of Hun invaders in the 6th century.

There was a further revival of Hindu power and culture under Harsha of Kanauj (606-647). During this period, central India was dominated by the Chalukya dynasty and the south by the Pallavas of Kanchi – but constant warfare led to division and sub-division of their empires. After the death of Harsha, kingdoms rose and fell in the north, and the whole continent fell into a state of anarchy which was exploited by Muslim invaders.

Muslim conquest
Though Sind had been conquered by the Muslims in the 8th century, the first major Islamic invasions were those of Mahmud of Ghazni between 1001 and 1026, again through the passes of the north-west frontier. These invasions were primarily looting expeditions, and it was not until the capture of Delhi by Muhammad of Ghur in 1192 that the way was open for Muslim conquest. Under successive rulers, the sultanate of Delhi spread across northern and central India, reducing existing rulers to the position of vassals.

But in the extreme south, the new Hindu empire of Vijayanagar arose from the confusion of conquest to threaten the stability of the sultanate. The empire survived until its destruction by the Muslims in 1565.

Empire of the Moguls
In 1526, Babur, a direct descendant of Tamerlane, defeated the reigning sultan of Delhi and founded the Mogul dynasty (Moghul is a form of the name Mongol). Babur's conquests were expanded and consolidated by his grandson, Akbar (1556-1605). The Moghul Empire, which was Muslim in religion, reached its greatest extent under Aurangzeb (1658 – 1707), when it covered most of India.

Under both the sultanate and the Moghul Empire considerable changes took place in northern and central India. New modes of thought and styles of art and architecture were introduced, and many Hindus were converted to Islam.

First Europeans
The Portuguese were the first Europeans to establish themselves in India. An expedition led by Vasco da Gama landed in western India in 1498, and by the mid-16th century the Portuguese had a firm foothold. Their main base was Goa.

Portuguese conquest was confined to small areas on the coast; its purpose was to secure the trade in spices and other luxuries for the European market.

The great profits made from the spice trade, as well as stories of the immense wealth of the Mogul emperors, attracted other Europeans. The first to break the Portuguese monopoly were the Dutch, closely followed by the British. London merchants founded the British East India Company in 1600. The French arrived in India in 1668.

By the mid-18th century the French and the British were contending for dominion in India. Mogul strength was collapsing in the face of both Hindu rebellion and a power struggle between Mogul provincial governors; the French and British supported the rival leaders as a front for their own ambitions.

Conquests of Clive
The true foundation of British dominion came with the victory of Robert Clive at Plassey in 1757, when he and his 3000 men defeated the Nawab of Bengal, whose army of 50,000 was supported by a small contingent of French artillerymen. The conflict between the Nawab and the British had begun with a British refusal to dismantle their fortifications at Calcutta. In June 1756, the Nawab seized the town and captured a number of European men, women and children. One hundred and forty-six of the prisoners were confined overnight in a small airless room – this was the notorious 'Black Hole of Calcutta', from which only 23 survived.

Clive's victory led to British control of Bengal, and this position was consolidated by Warren Hastings, who succeeded him as governor. By 1805 the British had extended their rule in both the north and south of India. Delhi was captured in 1803, and the Mogul ruler became a British puppet. This process continued until all the states were brought under British control, though some were left with a large measure of autonomy under their traditional rulers.

Indian Mutiny: 1857
Until 1858, the government of India was controlled not by the British Crown but by the East India Company – though from 1773 onwards the activities of the company itself were under the supervision of a British cabinet minister.

In 1857 the soldiers of the East India Company's Bengal army – Hindus, mostly, and Muslims – rebelled. They feared that their British officers were deliberately undermining their religion and trying to make them all Christians.

At first the mutineers were successful. They occupied Delhi and laid siege to Cawnpore and Lucknow. Taken by surprise, the British in India faced annihilation. But the arrival of reinforcements enabled them to crush the mutiny 14 months after it had broken out. Bloody reprisals were taken against the mutineers.

After the mutiny, the British government assumed direct responsibility for the government of India, the East India Company was abolished, and the governor-general was given the title of Viceroy. Social reforms which might have offended the religious beliefs of the masses were either abandoned or carried through in watered-down form.

Railways link the Raj
The British Raj (as British rule came to be called, after a Hindu word meaning 'to rule') now concentrated on the material progress of India. Railway construction, which had begun in 1853, was stepped up after 1869. By the end of the century the system was virtually complete, with nearly 35,000 miles of track – the largest railway system in Asia. New canals, too, were built, particularly in the Punjab and Sind, as part of a

full-scale campaign against famine. British imperialism reached the apogee of its expression with the proclamation and crowning of Queen Victoria as Empress of India in the year 1876.

Indian National Congress: 1885-1905
The frustration of the Indian middle classes led to the formation of the Indian National Congress in 1885 by university-educated Indians. Its aim was a moderate one – a fuller share in the running of the country. Some minor concessions were made, but the slowness with which even these were granted led to a split in Congress itself. Two rival groups emerged: the Moderates believed in pressing their case constitutionally, while the Extremists argued that by appealing to India's past they could arouse a revolutionary fervour in the masses.

The division of the unwieldy province of Bengal in 1905 by the ruling Viceroy, Lord Curzon, led to violent unrest. The British responded with concessions. In 1909, as part of the reforms introduced by John Morley, Secretary of State for India, the Legislative Council of the Viceroy, Lord Minto, was expanded to include 25 elected Indian members. Bengal was re-united in 1911. But the Moderates had lost their dominant position in Congress, which now started to build up a mass following and to become more militant.

Coming of the Mahatma
The outbreak of the First World War in 1914 produced a resurgence of loyalty. Over 500,000 Indians served in the Indian Army. But as the war dragged on, nationalist activity revived. The British conceded a measure of representative government through elected provincial officials by the Government of the India Act of 1919. But before this act came into force, circumstances in India had changed.

A new leader, Mahatma Gandhi (1869-1948), had emerged and his views strongly influenced the direction of Congress. Gandhi urged his followers to embark on a series of hartals (general strikes) and these soon led to violence in the Punjab, especially in Amritsar. In April 1919 British troops opened fire without warning on a mass street meeting in the city: 379 Indians were killed and over 1200 wounded. As a result, Gandhi changed his aims and now declared that India must throw off British rule completely.

Road to freedom: 1920-47
Under the influence of the Mahatma, Congress became a mass party, basing its support on the Hindu majority. Gandhi's method of Satyagraha (non-violent non-cooperation), used against the British, led to further bloodshed, particularly between Hindus and Muslims. His partner in the leadership was Pandit Jawaharlal Nehru (1889–1964), a westernised Brahmin (a member of the highest priestly caste of the Hindus), who gave Congress the image of a forward-looking, liberal-democratic party, with a socialist bias.

Under the pressure of mass civil disobedience, the British granted responsible parliamentary governments to the provinces of British India. But in October 1939, the Congress ministers resigned in protest at the unilateral declaration of war on Germany by the Viceroy. In 1942 a civil disobedience campaign escalated into open armed rebellion after the arrest of the principal Congress leaders.

In 1945 the British Labour Government's efforts to transfer power to a united India failed when the Muslim League – formed in 1906 to protect the interests of the Muslim minority in predominantly Hindu India – insisted on partition. Violence and anarchy grew, and in August 1947 the last Viceroy, Lord Mountbatten, finally handed over power to the two separate new states of the sub-continent, India and Pakistan.

First years of independence
Partition brought immediate bloodshed; in the Punjab alone, at least 600,000 were killed. Millions of Hindus were trapped in a hostile Muslim Pakistan, while the same fate overtook Muslims

in India. Some 14 million people are believed to have migrated between India and Pakistan.

The two new countries quarrelled over Kashmir, which, like the other princely states, had been given the option of joining either country. Its maharajah, a Hindu, ruled over a Muslim majority, and after a Muslim uprising the maharajah decided that his state should join India. But Pakistan claimed that Kashmir rightfully belonged to it, and war broke out between India and Pakistan. After renewed conflict, both sides agreed in 1966 to withdraw their troops behind a cease-fire line. Pakistan was left in control of the area north-west of this line, but India maintained its claim to the entire state.

India was also shaken by the assassination of Mahatma Gandhi by a Hindu extremist in January 1948. In the first elections held under universal suffrage in 1951, Congress gained an overwhelming majority.

Age of Nehru: 1947-64
The first prime minister of independent India in 1947 was Pandit Nehru, whom Gandhi had declared his political heir-apparent. Nehru declared that his principal aim was to modernise India, and especially to modify the caste system. New heavy industries were set up under state ownership. But as a result, agriculture was neglected, making India dependent for its food supplies on massive imports of grain.

When India became a republic in 1950 Nehru insisted that it remain a member of the British Commonwealth. Nehru's policy of 'non-alignment' with the superpowers of East and West went unchallenged as long as it brought advantages to India.

Despite the considerable social changes under Nehru, the last years of his life saw dissatisfaction at the failure of Congress to achieve major social and economic reforms.

Split in congress
Nehru was succeeded by Lal Bahadur Shastri. His period of office was short: it was dominated by a short war with Pakistan in September 1965, and ended by his death in January 1966. Shastri was succeeded by Mrs Indira Gandhi, Nehru's daughter. Her appointment was intended to revive the flagging image of Congress; but in the 1967 elections the party, though keeping its majority in the central parliament, lost heavily in the states. Continuous friction between Mrs Gandhi and the other leading figures of her party ended in a split in 1969. Because she lacked an adequate parliamentary majority, Mrs Gandhi called a general election in 1971. Her overwhelming victory gave Congress an absolute majority in the central parliament and the control of many states. The size of the vote was a sign of protest against the anarchy which had long reigned in Indian political life and had been intensified after the split in Congress.

War with Pakistan
By the winter of 1971, however, India had again become embroiled in war with Pakistan. Indian forces entered East Pakistan to help the oppressed Hindus, 6 million of whom had already fled into India. After overcoming Pakistani resistance, India supported the people of East Pakistan in setting up a new independent state of Bangladesh.

In June 1975, after a court ruled that Mrs Gandhi had violated election laws, the prime minister declared a state of emergency, suspended civil liberties and brought in censorship; 28,836 political opponents were arrested and jailed 'to save India from anarchy'. During the 19 months of the state of emergency, in an effort to reduce the birth rate, the government launched a vigorous sterilisation programme and raised the minimum marriage age. Mrs Gandhi and her Congress Party were resoundingly defeated in elections held in March 1977.

Restoration to power
The new government under Morarji Desai of the Janata Party, who had been imprisoned for 18 months under the state of emergency, set about restoring fundamental rights. Mrs Gandhi

had been ousted from the Congress Party and formed a party of her own – Congress-I (for Indira). It was this party that brought her back to office in 1980 when it won a landslide victory. In the next four years, to strengthen government control over business, Mrs Gandhi nationalised six of the country's largest banks, and parliament voted her government sweeping powers to arrest without warrant strikers in essential services.

In 1982 Mrs Gandhi and President Zia of Pakistan held the first meeting in 10 years between the leaders of the two nations. Fighting broke out in 1983 between Hindus and Muslims in the state of Assam – an estimated 5000 people were killed and a quarter of a million made homeless.

Sikh unrest
In 1982, Sikhs demanding autonomy for their state of Punjab attacked the parliament building in New Delhi. A year later Mrs Gandhi dismissed the Punjab state government and brought in direct rule from Delhi in an effort to end the strife between Hindus and Sikhs. In April and May of 1984 Sikhs demanding independence for a Sikh nation launched a series of attacks in the Punjab. To halt the violence, in June Indian troops fought their way into the centre of the Sikh religion, and

a stronghold, the Golden Temple of Amritsar. On October 31, 1984, Mrs Gandhi was gunned down by two Sikh members of her personal bodyguard. Her son Rajiv, who until 1980 had been an airline pilot, was sworn in as prime minister. His position was confirmed when the Congress-I Party had a landslide victory in the December elections and took 78.7 per cent of the seats up for election.

Bhopal tragedy
The worst industrial accident in history happened at Bhopal, in Madhya Pradesh, in December 1984 when a poison gas leak at the Union Carbide plant led to the deaths of 2000 people and injured an estimated 200,000.

Rajiv Gandhi said soon after he came to office that his aims were 'continuous modernisation, higher production and rapid advance of social justice'. He moved to improve efficiency within his own government and cut back the number of cabinet posts. His policy of moderation tempered extremist groups: in elections held in the Punjab in September 1985 it was the moderate Sikh Akali Dal party that won a sound majority rather than the extremists demanding an autonomous state.

In May 1991 Rajiv Gandhi was assassinated while campaigning for the election to be held later that month.

Nepal

This kingdom in the Himalayas has the world's highest peak, Mount Everest (8848 metres – 29,028 ft). Its tribal peoples include the Sherpas, famous as climbers, and the Gurkhas, whose fighting qualities have given them a unique place in military history.

Modern Nepal dates from 1768, when the small hill-state of Gurkha expanded over the whole area from Bhutan to Kashmir. In 1847 the Shah dynasty was reduced to figureheads by the aristocratic Ranas. In 1951 the Ranas, too, were ousted and a democratic constitution introduced. However, King Mahendra re-imposed direct rule in 1960, banning political parties. His son Birendra succeeded him on his death in 1972.

In 1990, after months of pro-democracy demonstrations, King Birendra dismissed the government and adopted a new constitution under which he no longer had absolute power.

NEPAL AT A GLANCE

Area 56,136 square miles

Population 17,420,000

Capital Kathmandu

Government Constitutional monarchy

Currency Rupee = 100 paisa

Languages Nepali and other local languages

Religions Hindu (90%), Buddhist, Muslim

Climate Temperate; average temperature in Kathmandu ranges from 2-23°C (36-73°F) in January to 20-29°C (68-84°C) in July

Main primary products Rice, wheat, barley, sugar cane, sorghum, cattle, medicinal herbs, jute, pepper, tobacco, fruit, timber

Major industries Agriculture, jute spinning, sugar milling, textiles, forestry, tourism

Main exports Rice and other farm products, timber, leather goods, jute, sugar, carpets

Annual income per head (US$) 166

Population growth (per thous/yr) 25

Life expectancy (yrs) Male 45 **Female** 44

Sri Lanka

An island off the subcontinent of India, formerly called Ceylon, Sri Lanka has long been affected by the proximity of its giant neighbour. The present population is descended mainly from Indian invaders; its principal religions are Buddhism and Hinduism, both carried south from India.

In the 16th century, Sri Lanka's abundance of spices began to attract traders from Europe. The island passed from Portuguese to Dutch and then to British control. It gained independence in 1948, and in 1960 became the world's first country to have a woman prime minister – Mrs Bandaranaike.

Conquerors from India
The first inhabitants were the Veddas, who emerged there c.3000 BC. They were conquered in the 6th century BC by invaders originating from northern India, and survive today only as a small group living in the remote interior. The invaders, the Sinhalese, at first inhabited northern Sri Lanka, where they laid out a complex irrigation system. They founded their capital at Anuradhapura, which became one of the major Buddhist centres of the Eastern world. Buddhism was the inspiration which brought about Sri Lanka's classical period of fine arts, between the 4th and 6th centuries AD.

Because Sri Lanka lay so close to India it was easily invaded, and the Sinhalese were followed in the 11th century

by another wave of invaders from India, the Hindu Tamils. By the 12th century, a Tamil kingdom had spread across the north of Sri Lanka and the Sinhalese had been driven into the south.

European control: 1505-1948
Sri Lanka's spices attracted Arab traders during the 12th and 13th centuries, and a prosperous trade developed. Descendants of the Arabs – the Muslim Moors – still live on the island.

The outward-looking Europeans of the 16th century were also lured by the profits to be made from spices. The first to arrive were the Portuguese, who from 1505 to 1597 controlled the whole island except the mountainous kingdom of Kandy.

The Dutch East India Company gained control in 1658, but the Dutch were forced out by the British in 1796. Throughout this time, Kandy remained a free kingdom, but in 1815 it, too, was overcome. The British introduced coffee, tea and rubber cultivation. Self-government was achieved gradually in the 20th century. In 1948 Sri Lanka gained full independence, but remained a member of the Commonwealth.

Independence
In 1956 the United National Party (UNP), the ruling party since independence, was beaten in elections; and the leader of the Sri Lanka Freedom party (SLFP), Solomon Bandaranaike, became prime minister – replacing Dudley Senanayake, the son of Sri Lanka's first prime minister. After this, the government's

policies became increasingly socialist.

Sri Lanka was shaken by bloody rioting in 1958 between Sinhalese and the Tamil minority – who make up 22 per cent of the population. The Tamils demanded recognition of their language as the alternative official tongue, and a separate Tamil state in a federal government. The prime minister was assassinated in 1959, and in 1960 his widow, Sirimavo Bandaranaike, became prime minister after an election victory.

Under the Bandaranaikes, Sri Lanka leaned towards the USSR and China, and expropriation of US oil companies without proper compensation caused the United States to suspend economic aid. The pro-Western Senanayake returned to power in 1965, but in 1970 Mrs Bandaranaike again became prime minister. After her defeat in 1977, the new pro-Western government, headed by J.R.Jayewardene, revised the constitution and established a strong presidential-parliamentary system.

President Jayewardene won re-election in October 1982 to a second six-year term. Ethnic relations between Tamils and Sinhalese dominated politics in Sri Lanka, and in July 1983 long-standing tensions between the two groups exploded. Violence spilled out of the north, where the indigenous Jaffna Tamils live, into the predominantly Sinhalese southern states. Relations with India, which has a large Tamil population, were

troubled as a result of the rioting and deaths of an estimated 400. The government declared a state of emergency but resisted the call for a separate Tamil state. The state of emergency ended in 1989, but the violence continued.

Maldives

Fishing and coconut growing are the chief industries on the Republic of Maldives, a cluster of coral islands south-west of Sri Lanka. The population is almost entirely Muslim.

In 1796 Britain took over Ceylon (now Sri Lanka) from the Dutch, along with the Maldives, which were under Ceylon's

protection. Ceylon became independent in 1948, but the British did not give the Maldives freedom until 1965. A republic was proclaimed in 1968 under President Amir Ibrahim Nasir. President Nasir suspended the constitution and ruled by decree until he resigned in 1978. Maumoon Abdul Gayoom was elected president in 1978, 1983 and 1988. A coup was staged in November 1988, but failed to oust the government.

Pakistan

Following Britain's withdrawal in 1947, the Indian subcontinent was partitioned into two states: Pakistan, predominantly Muslim, and India, mainly Hindu. Pakistan itself was divided into eastern and western 'wings', separated by more than 1000 miles of Indian territory. The new state lasted in this form for only 25 years. The east broke away in 1971, and in 1972 became the republic of Bangladesh.

Muslim conquest
An Arab army conquered the Indian kingdom of Sind (today a province of Pakistan) in the 8th century AD, but it was not until the invasions by the Turks in the 11th and 12th centuries that Islam became firmly established in northern India.

The power of the Muslim sultanate, centred on Delhi, soon spread throughout northern India, and by 1320 it had reached the far south. But in 1398 the Tatar conqueror Tamerlane sacked Delhi, and the sultanate broke up into a number of small Muslim kingdoms.

In 1526 a new Muslim conqueror appeared on the Indian scene. Babur, a descendant of Tamerlane and Genghis Khan, defeated the reigning sultan, Ibrahim Lodi, at the battle of Panipat and set himself on the throne. Because of his ancestry, his dynasty took the name Mogul (Mongol).

Internal revolt in the early 18th century so weakened the empire that it fell – first to Hindu warriors, the Marathas, and then to the British. With British expansion in India, Mogul power came to an end; the last emperor was deposed in 1859.

Muslim rebirth and growth of separatism
After the failure of the Indian Mutiny (1857-9), the position of Indian Muslims became much worse. Though the mutiny had been started by Hindus, the British believed that it had been a Muslim attempt to restore the Mogul Empire, and made it clear

that Muslims would not be trusted in positions of responsibility. The Muslim response was to strengthen their faith, as a symbol of solidarity. After the great upsurge of Hindu nationalism created by resentment at the partition of Bengal by the British in 1905, it was decided to grant all Indians the right to some share in government. But the fear of Hindu domination alarmed the Muslims, and they demanded safeguards in the form of separate Muslim constituencies. These demands were accepted, and a political party known as the Muslim League was founded in 1906.

Creation of Pakistan
Muhammad Ali Jinnah (1876–1948) began his political life as a member of the Indian National Congress. At first he was a believer in Hindu-Muslim unity, though he insisted on proper safeguards for the Muslim minority. He broke with Congress, however, disagreeing with Ghandi's policy of non-cooperation with the British. In 1935, after the announcement that parliaments were to be set up in all the provinces of British India, he led the Muslim League in its election battle. The League's showing was only modest, and the victorious Congress Party rejected an offer of cooperation by Jinnah. As a result, Jinnah proclaimed his goal to be the creation of Pakistan.

Throughout the negotiations with the British over the transfer of power in India, Jinnah maintained his stand. In June 1947 the British government agreed to his demands and handed over power to two new states – Pakistan and India. Pakistan came into being as an independent nation within the British Commonwealth on August 14, 1947, with Jinnah as governor-general and Liaquat Ali Khan as prime minister. The division of British India meant that millions of both Hindus and Muslims were left in the 'wrong' country. At least 600,000 people died in clashes between Hindus and Muslims, while 14 million more were uprooted from their homes, to stream over the borders as refugees.

SRI LANKA AT A GLANCE
Area 25,332 square miles
Population 16,810,000
Capital Colombo
Government Parliamentary republic
Currency Sri Lankan rupee = 100 cents
Languages Sinhala (official), Tamil, English
Religions Buddhist (69%), Hindu (15.5%), Muslim (7.7%), Christian (7.5%)
Climate Tropical; temperatures range from 23-31°C (73-88°F) in Colombo and from 14-24°C (57-75°F) in the highlands
Main primary products Rice, coconuts, tea, rubber, cassava, fruit, spices, timber, fish; gemstones and semiprecious stones (sapphire, ruby, beryl, topaz, spinel, garnet, moonstone), iron ore, graphite
Major industries Agriculture, textiles, mining, forestry, fishing, oil refining
Main exports Tea, rubber, coconut products, textiles, gemstones, petroleum products
Annual income per head (US$) 367
Population growth (per thous/yr) 18
Life expectancy (yrs) Male 67 **Female** 71

MALDIVES AT A GLANCE
Area 115 square miles
Population 214,100
Capital Malé
Government Republic
Currency Rufiyaa = 100 laari
Languages Divehi (a form of Sinhalese), English
Religion Muslim
Climate Tropical; average temperature ranges from 25°C (77°F) to 29°C (84°F)
Main primary products Fish, fruit, vegetables, coconuts
Major industries Fishing, agriculture
Main exports Canned, processed fish
Annual income per head (US$) 410
Population growth (per thous/yr) 30
Life expectancy (yrs) Male 46 **Female** 48

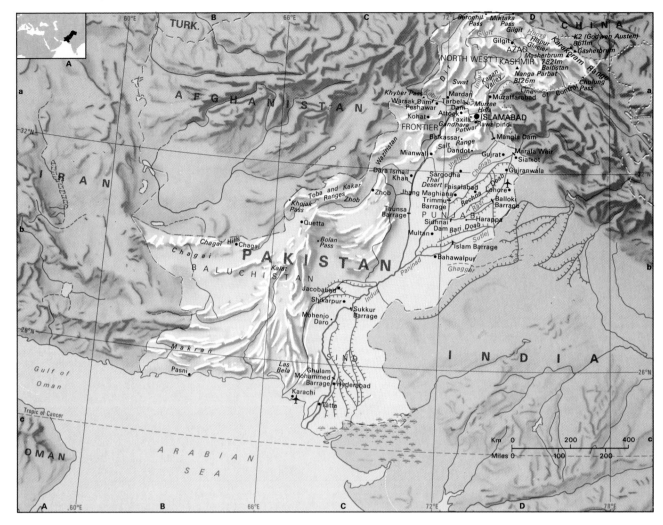

PAKISTAN AT A GLANCE
Area 310,402 square miles
Population 105,400,000
Capital Islamabad
Government Federal Islamic republic
Currency Pakistani rupee
Languages Urdu, English, Punjabi, Sindhi, Pushtu, Baluchi, Bravi
Religions Muslim (97%), Hindu (1.6%), Christian (1.4%)
Climate Subtropical; monsoon from June to October. Average temperature in Karachi ranges from 13-25°C (55-77°F) in January to 28-34°C (82-93°F) in June
Main primary products Cotton, wheat, rice, sugar cane, maize, fruit (dates), tobacco; natural gas, gypsum, iron ore (also bauxite, copper, antimony, magnesite, phosphates – not yet exploited)
Major industries Agriculture, cotton yarn and fabrics, sports goods, petroleum refining, cement, sugar refining, fertilisers, food processing
Main exports Cotton and cotton textiles, rice, hand-crafted carpets and guns, sports goods, leather goods, petroleum products
Annual income per head (US$) 354
Population growth (per thous/yr) 30
Life expectancy (yrs) Male 51 **Female** 50

From partition onwards, India and Pakistan disputed the fate of Kashmir, which lay on the border between them. It had a predominantly Muslim population, but its Hindu ruler chose to join India. Late in 1947 an undeclared war was fought there between the Indian and Pakistani armies. It was temporarily settled by the division of Kashmir along a cease-fire line.

Politics and war: 1947-65
After the death of Jinnah in 1948 and the assassination of Liaquat Ali Khan in 1951, the precarious control of the new government gradually disintegrated. In September 1954 the government declared a state of emergency and dissolved the National Assembly. After two years of deliberation, a new constitution was adopted making Pakistan an Islamic republic, General Iskandar Mirza became its first president.

In October 1958 Mirza abolished political parties and declared martial law. Three weeks later Mirza himself was overthrown by the army, and his palace was taken by General Ayub Khan. A new constitution was introduced, and Ayub, ending martial law, became president. Pakistan, however, remained dominated by its army. Though Pakistan's relations with India gradually improved, the question of Kashmir was a running sore. War finally broke out between Pakistan and India in September 1965. It was short and inconclusive; by the Tashkent Agreement both sides pledged themselves to return to the positions they had held before the war.

East Pakistan breaks away
Strikes, riots, assassinations and demands for democratic elections led to the fall of Ayub Khan in 1969. He was replaced by General Yahya Khan. Yahya announced that general elections would be held in 1970 and a new constitution introduced by January 1971.

In the east, the result of the elections was an overwhelming majority for Sheikh Mujibur Rahman and his Awami League. Mujibur had made it clear that his party wanted an end to East Pakistan's political status as a 'poor relation', when, in fact, it produced much of the country's revenue. Politicians in the west, such as Zulfikar Ali Bhutto, urged Yahya to stop Sheikh Mujibur from taking office. After talks between Yahya and Mujibur failed, units of the army were sent to the east to impose martial law. The crisis worsened during 1971, and East Pakistan proclaimed itself an independent republic – Bangladesh. West Pakistani troops went to extreme lengths to crush the secessionists. But India intervened and Pakistan lost the war. Yahya resigned and Bhutto took his place.

Martial Law and after
Controversial elections in 1977 threw Pakistan into civil turmoil. Bhutto announced that his Pakistan People's Party (PPP) had won a landslide victory but opponents declared the election had been stolen by fraud. General Mohammad Zia ul-Haq, chief of staff of the army, seized control of the government, arresting Bhutto and imposing martial law. Bhutto was convicted on charges of murder and hanged despite pleas for clemency from world leaders. After scheduling a national election for November 1979, Zia cancelled it, banned political activities and arrested hundreds of politicians. Pakistan was torn by riots throughout 1983 as opponents led demonstrations against Zia's martial law government. When a general election was held in 1985, seven of Zia's ministers were defeated.

In August 1988 Zia was killed in a plane crash. In November that year elections were held and Benazir Bhutto, the daughter of Zulfikar Ali Bhutto, led the PPP to victory. In 1990 Benazir Bhutto and her cabinet were dismissed amid allegations of corruption.

Burma

An independent republic since 1948, when it left the British Commonwealth, Burma has in recent years tried to follow a policy of strict neutrality; its economy has stagnated under an isolationist socialist-military regime.

The original homeland of the Burmese was the present upper Burma, centred on Mandalay. The Burmese gradually expanded, conquering and absorbing the Mon peoples of lower Burma, and subduing, but not assimilating, various people of the hill areas, such as the Shans, Karens, and the coastal Arakanese.

Early kingdoms
The earliest state in Burma flourished in the 7th and 8th centuries AD around its capital city of Srikshetra, some distance north of modern Rangoon. Its people, called the Pyu, were Hindus and used the Sanskrit language. In the 11th century the people from whom the modern Burmese are descended conquered their non-Burmese neighbours and established a kingdom that lasted 200 years. A Burmese king, Anawratha, introduced Buddhism, which is still the main religion of the country – 85 per cent of Burmese are Buddhists.

The drive to unity: 1301-1824
Several independent states emerged in the 14th century. The Burmese established the city of Ava, in the north, while the Mons built Pegu in the south. A third people, the Shans, captured Ava in 1527: but further south, at Toungoo, a new Burmese state had been evolving, and it seized control of Pegu in 1539 and conquered many of the Shan territories. The Burmese thenceforward dominated the country, despite a Mon revolt against them in 1740.

Anglo-Burmese wars: 1824-85
Frontier tension between Burma and British India led to a war in 1824-6, ending with the British annexation of the provinces of Tenasserim and Arakan. British trading ambitions, which caused bitterness between the Burmese and British merchants in the country, led to a second war in 1852-4. As a result, lower Burma, including Rangoon, became a British province. Finally, in 1885, after a third war, the British took over the rest of Burma.

Growth of nationalism: 1906-42
Burmese nationalism in its modern form began with the organisation from 1906 onwards of Young Men's Buddhist Associations. Buddhist monks played a leading part in the political activity of the 1920s, but in the 1930s the initiative passed to English-educated students, who organised a major strike in 1936. The British permitted some measure of constitutional development and in 1937 a Burmese cabinet with limited powers was formed.

Japanese occupation: 1942-5
The Japanese invaded Burma in 1942, forcing British withdrawal by May. In 1943, the Japanese proclaimed Burma's independence and set up a puppet government. But during 1945 Allied troops, mainly British, defeated the invaders. The Allies were assisted by the Burma National Army led by Aung San, previously supporters of the Japanese. Aung San formed an Anti-Fascist People's Freedom League (AFPFL) whose aim was to achieve independence.

Independence: 1948
In July 1947 Aung San was assassinated, and U Nu became prime minister of the independent Union of Burma in 1948. Independence was followed almost immediately by a series of revolts. Order was not restored for more than three years, and revolts continued through the 1950s. Nevertheless, a constitutional system was established in Rangoon, and U Nu won two successive elections.

Military rule: 1962
U Nu's regime was overthrown in 1962 by an army leader, General Ne Win. The new military government pursued the 'Burmese way to Socialism', and nationalised most industries and businesses. The military regime, which laid great stress on a neutralist foreign policy, and also rejected foreign private investment and aid, faced serious economic problems. In 1974 it adopted a new one-party constitution. Ne Win stepped down in 1981, but he remained a powerful figure behind the scenes.

Burma today
In 1988 millions of Burmese took to the streets in peaceful demonstrations for democracy. These were stopped when General Saw Maung seized power and imposed martial law. In 1989 the government changed the official name of the country to the Union of Myanmar.

The opposition National League for Democracy, led by Aung San's daughter, Aung San Suu Kyi, won a landslide majority in elections in May 1990. At first, the government said that it would hand over power but within six months most opposition leaders had been arrested, and power was still firmly in the hands of the army. In 1991, Aung San Suu Kyi, who had been under house arrest for more than a year, was awarded the Nobel Peace Prize.

The problem of Burma's minority peoples also remains unresolved, and intermittent fighting continues as some 20 different ethnic groups carry on warfare against the government.

BURMA AT A GLANCE
Area 261,217 square miles
Population 39,300,000
Capital Rangoon
Government One-party socialist republic
Currency Kyat = 100 pyas
Languages Burmese and tribal
Religion Buddhist
Climate Tropical; monsoon from May to September. Average temperature in Rangoon ranges from 18-32°C (64-90°F) in January to 24-36°C (75-97°F) in April
Main primary products Rice, sugar cane, groundnuts, jute, cotton, rubber, timber; oil and natural gas, lead, zinc, tungsten, nickel
Major industries Forestry, oil and gas production, mining, fishing, food processing, textiles
Main exports Rice, teak, jute, rubber
Annual income per head (US$) 200
Population growth (per thous/yr) 20
Life expectancy (yrs) Male 53 **Female** 56

Picture Credits

p.9 F. Kohler; p.10 top Trigalou-Pix; bottom Koch-Rapho; p.11 Gruyaert-Magnum; p.12 S. Held; p.12/13 Michaud-Rapho; p.13 S. Held; p.14 F. Kohler; p.15 F. Kohler; p.16 S. Held; p.17 top Trigalou-Pix; bottom F. Kohler; p.18 Gabanou-Diaf; p.19 Michaud-Rapho; p.20 left S. Held; right S. Held; p.21 F. Kohler; p.22 Shelley-Rapho; p.23 left Michaud-Rapho; right F. Kohler; p.24 F. Kohler; p.25 Trigalou-Pix; p.26 top Gruyaert-Magnum; bottom A. Hutchison Lby; p.27 Silverstone-Magnum; p.28 Villota-Image Bank; p.29 S. Held; p.30 Linnemann-Arepi; p.31 C. Lénars; p.32 Michaud-Rapho; p.33 S. Held; p.34 left C. Lénars; right C. Lénars; p.35 C. Lénars; p.36 P. Frillet; p.37 Michaud-Rapho; p.38 A. Hutchison Lby; p.39 top S. Held; bottom P. Frillet; p.40 S. Held; p.41 Grismayer-Pix; p.42 top C. Lénars; bottom A. Hutchison Lby; p.43 C. Lénars; p.44 S. Held; p. 45 top C. Lénars; bottom C. Lénars; p.46 A. Hutchison Lby; p. 47 A. Hutchison Lby; p.48 left S. Held; right C. Lénars; p.49 Singh-Ana; p. 50 F. Kohler; p.51 top J. Lamothe; bottom Garcin-Diaf; p.52 top C. Lénars; bottom C. Lénars; p.53 C. Lénars; p.54 Kérébel-Diaf; p.55 S. Held; p.56 S. Held; p.57 Singh-Ana; p.58 top F. Kohler; bottom A. Hutchison Lby; p.59 S. Held; p.60 C. Lénars; p.61 C. Lénars; p.62 Adamini-Gamma; p.63 top Jaffre-Durou; bottom Loieau-Diaf; p.64 Michaud-Rapho; p.65 S. Held; p.66 Le Querrec-Magnum; p.67 top Schoenahl-Diaf; bottom Schoenahl-Diaf; p.68 Singh-Ana; p.69 Pelletier-Cedri; p.70 Michaud-Rapho; p.71 left Michaud-Rapho; right Franck-Magnum; p.72 A. Hutchison Lby; p.73 C. Lénars; p.74 Petit-Top; p.75 top Pelletier-Cedri; bottom Petit-Top; p.76 Raynaud; p.77 Raynaud; p.78 Pelletier-Cedri; p.79 Page-A. Hutchison Lby; p.80 Shelley-Rapho; p.81 left

S. Held; right Charles-Rapho; p.82 S. Held; p.83 left S. Held; right S. Held; p.84 N. Singh; p.85 top N. Singh; bottom Pinsard-Cedri; p.86 Errington-A. Hutchison Lby; p.87 top Michaud-Rapho; bottom A. Hutchison Lby; p.88 C. Lénars; p.89 Bossu-Picat-Fotogram; p.90 A. & S. Mouraret; p.91 Weisbecker-Explorer; p.92 Weisbecker-Explorer; p.93 Thevenet-Pix; p.94 S. Held; p.95 G. Stein; p.96 Schoenahl-Diaf; p.97 Carot-Fotogram; p.98 Barbey-Magnum; p.99 top S. Held; bottom S. Held; p.100 S. Held; p.101 Barbey-Magnum; p.102 top Schoenahl-Diaf; bottom Neveu-Diaf; p.103 S. Held; p.104 top C. Lénars; bottom Giraud-Fotogram; p.105 S. Held; p.106 Trigalou-Pix; p.107 top Carot-Fotogram; bottom Barbey-Magnum; p.108 Dumas-Fotogram; p.109 J. Bottin; p.110 S. Held; p.111 left F. Kohler; right F. Kohler; p.112 Y. Travert; p.113 left Y. Travert; right S. Marmounier; p. 114 Frillet; p.115 top Mayer-Magnum; bottom S. Marmounier; p.116 left Sauvageot-Cedri; right Frillet; p.117 Barbey-Magnum; p.118 S. Held; p. 119 Barbey-Magnum; p.120 S. Held; p. 121 left Y. Travert; right A. Hutchison Lby; p.122 top Abbas-Gamma; bottom H. Granier; p.123 G. Blondeau; p.124 Y. Travert; p.125 H. Granier; p.126 Mouton-Cedri; p.127 left H. Granier; right H. Granier; p.128 H. Granier; p.129 Gérard-Explorer p.130 Durou-Jaffre; p.131 Garcin-Diaf; p.132 Schoenahl-Diaf; p.133 top Negre-Explorer; bottom Negre-Explorer; p.134 left Durou; right Reffet-Diaf; p.135 Reffet-Diaf; p.136 top Jules-Ana; bottom C. Lénars; p.137 Tatopoulos-Explorer; p.138 top L. Boucaud; bottom F. Kohler; p.139 Metha-Contact-Cosmos; p.140 Garcin-Diaf; p.141 Reffet-Diaf; p.142 Reffet-Diaf; p.143 Reffet-Diaf; p.144 Garcin-Diaf; p.145 left Reffet-Diaf; right Reffet-Diaf; p.146 Reffet-Diaf; p.147 top F. Kohler; bottom Reffet-Diaf;

p.148 Durou; p.149 Veiller-Explorer; p. 150 Barbey-Magnum; p.151 S. Held; p.152 Barbey-Magnum; p.153 left S. Held; right Barbey-Magnum; p. 154 top Muller-Cedri; bottom S. Held; p.155 Muller-Cedri; p.156 top A. Boucaud; bottom C. Lénars; p.157 Muller-Cedri; p.158 Veiller-Explorer; p 159 Barbier-Diaf; p.160 top Barbey-Magnum; bottom Barbey-Magnum; p.161 Grey-Gamma; p.162 Muller-Cedri; p.163 left D. Jeu; right D. Jeu; p.164 Huguler-Explorer; p.165 Villota-Image Bank; p.166 Barbier-Diaf; p.167 left Veiller-Explorer; p.168 right S. Held; p.169 S. Held

Cover pictures:
Top: F. Wing-Image Bank
Bottom: B. Barbey-Magnum

74-010-1